MOECK

The Authors

Ray Robinson is Professor of music and President of Westminster Choir College in Princeton, New Jersey (USA), an appointment he has held since 1969. He is a violist and the author of articles and books on choral music and church music.

Allen Winold is Professor of music theory at Indiana University in Bloomington, Indiana. He is also a conductor and violist and the author of a number of books on music.

© 1983 by Moeck Verlag + Musikinstrumentenwerk, D-3100 Celle
All rights reserved
Printed in the Federal Republic of Germany
Ed. Moeck No. 4026 · ISBN 3-87549-016-9

Ray Robinson
Allen Winold

A Study of the Penderecki
St. Luke Passion

Ed. Moeck No. 4026

MOECK VERLAG · CELLE

TABLE OF CONTENTS

Acknowledgments

The authors wish to express appreciation to a number of individuals who provided help in the preparation and completion of this book. Acknowledgment is due, first and foremost, to the composer and his wife, Elizabeth, for their assistance in so many ways, not the least of which was finding time in a busy schedule for meetings in New York, Aspen, Krakow, Chicago, Assisi, Baltimore, Philadelphia and Berlin. Without the help of Steven Demorest, Catherine Le Duc, and Kirsten Olson in research, proofreading and technical bibliographical matters and of Laura Van Horn in professional advice and manuscript preparation, this project could not have been completed on schedule.

Special acknowledgement is due to Dr. Reinhold Quandt, Verlagsleiter at Moeck Verlag, Celle, West Germany, for his kindness and hospitality during the period of research.

Finally, the authors would like to thank Ronald Freed, European American Music Distributors Corporation, and Jacques Leiser, the composer's American representative, for their encouragement and support.

The Authors

Introduction

This study of the *St. Luke Passion* by the contemporary Polish composer Krzysztof Penderecki is written for both musical amateurs and professional musicians. It is one of the interesting paradoxes of works such as these that a knowledge of traditional music literature and theory, while helpful, is not a prerequisite to understanding the music, for much of it is based upon musical materials and techniques that are new to the professional as well as the amateur.

Each of the seven chapters of the book explores a different aspect of the work. Chapter I considers the work in the context of the life of its composer; it describes the first performance in 1966 and discusses the world-wide reaction to the premiere and subsequent performances and recordings. The second chapter considers the work in the context of the history of musical settings of the Passion story. The third chapter considers the textual sources for the work and presents an outline of the dramatic structure of the Passion as set by Penderecki.

The last four chapters focus on the musical content of the work; each one views it from a different point of view. Chapter IV covers general aspects of the music, such as vocal and instrumental setting and techniques, concepts and notation of rhythm and pitch, musical sources, and larger formal aspects. Chapter V is devoted to detailed descriptions of the individual movements of the Passion. These are written in outline form and include the full text in Latin, and brief descriptions of the text setting, timbre, texture, and themes. Short commentaries following each movement cover special points of interest, outline the formal organization of the movement, and discuss its relation to other movements. This is the longest chapter of the book and it may be used as a guide for listening or score study.

Chapter VI considers the important topic of pitch relations in the work. Though intended to be of special interest to professional readers, it should also be accessible and interesting for the amateur. It includes brief explanations of some modern analytical methods, which are especially appropriate for this work. The final chapter is devoted to a comparison of this work to works of other composers and to earlier works by Pendercki.

Penderecki's *St. Luke Passion* has been recognized as one of the most significant choral works of the second half of this century and has been widely discussed in articles and books published in Europe. It is the hope of the authors that this first full length study of the work in English will contribute to a fuller understanding and an appreciation of this monumental work.

The Passion is the suffering and death of Christ, but it is also the suffering and death at Auschwitz, the tragic experience of mankind in the middle of the twentieth century. In this sense, it should, according to my intentions and feelings, have a universal, humanistic character like *Threnody*[1].

Krzysztof Penderecki, 1966

Chapter I

KRZYSZTOF PENDERECKI AND THE ST. LUKE PASSION

The world premiere of the *St. Luke Passion* on March 30, 1966 at the Cathedral of Münster (West Germany) brought the thirty-two year-old composer Krzysztof Penderecki the kind of immediate acclaim that is unusual in the field of concert music. There have been few composers in the history of music who have enjoyed so swift a rise to world prominence. Prior to the performance of *St. Luke* he was known outside his native Poland primarily on the basis of his success with the orchestral pieces *Anaklasis* and *Threnody*. Afterward he was the beneficiary of a worldwide platform that assured performances, recordings, and publications of almost any work he would write.

The very fact that a product of the *avant garde* could emerge from a socialist country, that had been in virtual isolation from the rest of western European culture since the end of the second world war, and produce a major work for chorus and orchestra was news indeed. But what really captured the imagination of the press and public alike was the thought that it would be possible for a composer to emerge from an eastern bloc country and write a successful musical composition on a Biblical text. For after all, not since 1803 had an important work been written for orchestra and chorus on the topic of the Passion. And, ironically, it was also a thirty-two year old composer who produced this nineteenth century work. His name? Ludwig van Beethoven (1770-1827). The work? *Christus am Ölberg* (Christ on the Mount of Olives).[2]

The factors that made the Penderecki premiere such an important event were not only of a political and social nature, however. No other composer since Johann Sebastian Bach (1685-1750) had captured the dramatic intent and the musical essence of the Passion story in the way Penderecki had. And it had been accomplished in the compositional idiom of the *avant garde*. The *St. Luke Passion* was indeed a twentieth century Passion, a legitimate contemporary expression that overwhelmed its hearers and convinced them that even in a modern setting this 2,000-year-old text still contained the same mystery and drama that moved men and women during the earliest years of the Church. The obvious musical craftsmanship of the work, combined with the fact that here was a courageous young composer dealing with a topic that was forbidden by his government, made the *St. Luke Passion* all the more appealing to the protest-minded musical public of the mid-1960s.

While there were some detractors, on balance the Penderecki *Passion* was viewed as one of the major achievements of the twentieth century. The German critic Wolfram Schwinger called the date of the premiere "one of the most significant dates of world music history". The critical acclaim the work received following its first performance is a matter of public record.

It is the purpose of this chapter to place the *St. Luke Passion* in its proper historical context. We will begin by discussing some of the reasons the composer selected a Biblical text.

At first glance, it seems unusual that a contemporary Polish composer would choose a Biblical text for his first large choral work. However, the more one studies the history of this eastern European country, the less surprising Penderecki's interest in religious text becomes. For after all, Penderecki is a Pole and he is best understood within this context.

Poles are a people who have refused to turn their backs on a tradition and a heritage of more than a thousand years, even if the prevailing political climate seems to forbid free artistic and religious expression. The Polish tradition is a history of a people rather than of a national state; as such it is based on cultural ties rather than racial ones or national goals. The Polish spirit, of which Penderecki is typical, reflects the attitudes and reactions which set Poles apart and differentiate them from those who come from other national backgrounds. One of the most important of these national characteristics, and one which is consistent throughout Penderecki's career as a composer, is the acceptance and continued practice of Christianity.

The one cardinal element which has always stood high and above all others in Poland, and explains why Penderecki chose a Biblical text for this important commission, is the role Christianity has played throughout the country's long history of foreign rule and occupation. The very establishment of the Polish state is closely linked with Poland's first king, Mieszko, who was baptized into the Christian faith in 966 (a date that should not be overlooked when considering that the first performance of the Penderecki *St. Luke Passion* took place in 1966). Significant also is the fact that Mieszko accepted Christianity in its Latin form and thus determined that Poland's future history would develop closely with that of Western civilization. Culturally, this decision isolated Poland from other eastern European countries and definitely separated Poles culturally from their Slavic neighbors to the East, the Russians, who had accepted Christianity in its Greek form.

The ideals which were introduced by the Church in Poland's early years found ready minds as well as willing hearts in the people and thus became a creative force in the development of the state. By this dual attachment to the spiritual ideals of Christianity and the political traditions of the West, the Polish people became conscious of their geographical position and were forced to defend and cling tenaciously to their language, customs and social institutions lest they be absorbed or affected by their bordering neighbors who had established a different way of life. This close personal bond between the Church and its members was a lifelong one; it baptized at birth, confirmed in childhood, married at adulthood, and buried after death. In the period since World War II, the Church and the people have again been brought together in resistance. The citizenry, about ninety-five percent Catholic, cling tenaciously to their faith and the constant governmental attacks on the Church only serve to strengthen their religious convictions.

Penderecki's selection of a Latin text from one of the four gospels for this work commissioned by the West German Radio to commemorate the 700th anniversary of the Cathedral of Münster was thus very much in the Polish tradition. For Poles the *St. Luke Passion* became a rallying point as the young composer exhibited the courage to write a musical work on a subject that was forbidden by the State. Perhaps doubting the personal religious convictions of the composer, a reporter asked Penderecki at the press conference which took place on the day of the premiere if he was a believing Catholic. He replied: "Ja, ein gläubiger linksorthodoxer Katholik" ("Yes, a believing liberal Catholic").[3] By so doing, he examplified another Polish trait: the courage to speak out and to avoid compromise on fundamental issues.

As far as the selection of St. Luke over the other acounts of the Passion story is concerned, there is no question but that the Bach Passions were critical in this decision. When asked at the same press conference why he had chosen St. Luke over the other gospels, Penderecki replied: "Not only for literary reasons, on account of the especially beautiful language, but rather because there had already been two unusually good Passion compositions based on Matthew and John."[4] This debt to the great Baroque master is made explicit not only in the sellection of the text, but also through the use of the BACH motive which is skillfully woven into the harmonic and melodic texture of the work.

We will now turn to Penderecki's early years and the events that led to the composition of the *St. Luke Passion*.

Student Years in Dębica and Krakow

Penderecki's formative years were spent in a small Polish town during a period of national suffering and political turmoil. Born on November 23, 1933, in the provincial city of Dębica[5], he had been an eye-witness to the devastating effects of both the German occupation and Communist domination. The atrocities of Auschwitz took place in his own back yard, and the final years of Stalinist oppression were a vivid experience of his teenage years. Since he lived in Poland during this period, he experienced first-hand the horror and terror of the times. These events could not help but heighten his social consciousness and shape his highly charged, intensely emotional scores.

Because he was raised in a devout Roman Catholic home, religion rather than music dominated his early life. "Until I was fifteen I was perhaps overly devout," Penderecki told an interviewer for *Newsweek* magazine in 1969. "I had begun reading Augustine and Aquinas. My mother wanted me to go into the church. In our town the Church was absolutely the center of life. People would kiss the shoulder of the priest as he walked by."[6] And so it was in a small Polish town during his childhood years.

Penderecki's musical interests were nurtured in early childhood by a family in which music occupied an important place. His father, Tadeusz, a lawyer by profession, was an avid musical amateur and enthusiastic chamber music player. His mother Zofia was a singer. With the encouragement of his parents, he studied both the piano and the violin. While there were no professional musicians in the family, nevertheless a great deal of amateur music making occurred in the home while he was still a young boy. His father and various uncles played duets and quartets during their leisure hours. With the passing years Penderecki's attachment to the violin became more serious while his interest in the piano waned.

Upon the completion of basic schooling in his home town, Penderecki went to Krakow in 1951 to enter the university and to study art, literature and philosophy. His interest focused on classical antiquity, the study of Greek, Latin and philosophy. Parallel to his university studies ran his musical training at the Krakow Conservatory. Here he resumed the violin studies he had begun after the war, and he made his first informal attempts at composition. His teachers at the Conservatory were Stanislaw Tawroszewicz, with whom he studied violin privately, and Franciszek Skolyszewski, who gave Penderecki a fundamental background in music theory. Skolyszewski was his first important compositional influence, a fact noted in a 1968 interview in which he cited his personal debt to Skolyszewski: "I owe my entire musical development to him, for it was he who discovered my talent and encouraged me."[7]

With the support of his teacher and with the growing realization that he had something important to say as a composer, Penderecki abandoned his university studies in 1954 to enter the State Academy of Music in Krakow to pursue serious training for a career as a composer. He studied at the Academy for four years. After the first year, however, he gave up the violin and dedicated himself completely to the study of composition. His principal teacher was Artur Malawski (1904-1957), a student of Kazimierz Sikorski (*1895), and he had taught at the Academy since 1945. Malawski, a major influence on the young Penderecki, was an adventurous composer who was able to maintain a healthy balance between contemporary techniques and tradition. He was regarded as one of the most important Polish composers after Szymanowski. He was also active in the International Society for Contemporary Music (ISCM) and led the Polish section of that organization between 1948 and 1951.

Acknowledging his indebtedness to Malawski some years later, Penderecki echoed his teacher's compositional philosophy when he stated: "The general principles at the root of a work's musical style, the logic and economy of development, and the integrity of a musical experience embodied in the notes the composer is setting down on the paper, never change. The idea of good music means today exactly what it meant always."[8] It is obvious that tradition is important to Penderecki, as exemplified by the *homage* to J. S. Bach in the *St. Luke Passion*, and it is clear that Malawski was a key influence in the development of the young composer's sense of tradition.

After Malawski's death in 1957, Penderecki studied for a short time with Stanislaw Wiechowicz (1893-1963), who was known in Poland as a composer of large choral works. However, in reality he hardly worked with Wiechowicz at all. Instead, during this final year at the Academy, he pursued his compositional craft alone and prepared for his graduation examinations. During these student years Penderecki composed some conservative works for small ensembles, "Two Songs for Baritone" on poems of Leopold Staff (1955-58), a string quartet (1955-57), and a set of *Three Miniatures for Clarinet and Piano* (1956) that later became his earliest published work (Polskie Wydawnictwo Muzyczne, 1958). He also wrote, as a memorial to his teacher, his first large work for orchestra, entitled "Epitaph on the Death of Malawski" (1958). This two-movement instrumental requiem for string orchestra and timpani was premiered in June 1958 in a concert of the Krakow Philharmonic under Michael Barnowski. With the success of the "Epitaph" as his final graduation requirement, Penderecki was now ready to pursue an active career as a composer.

One of the amazing aspects of Penderecki's student years in Krakow (1951-58) was that he lived, studied and composed in virtual isolation from the outside musical world. This almost complete absence from Western compositional influences was undoubtedly a decisive factor in the highly original musical language that he later developed. For example, he heard the Stravinsky *Rite of Spring* for the first time in 1957, at the first Warsaw Autumn Festival, only one year before graduating from the Academy. His initial contact with the music of the Viennese School of Schönberg, Berg and Webern occurred one year later when Luigi Nono (*1924) and his wife Nurva (the daughter of Arnold Schoenberg) visited Poland for the purpose of introducing this music, along with the works of Nono, to the Polish workers. Schönberg's *Five Pieces for Orchestra* and *De Profundis* and Webern's cantata *Das Augenlicht* and the *String Quartet* were among the scores Penderecki came to know and study as the result of Nono's visit. Some years later he stated that some of his early works - among them *Strophes* and *Emanations* - were influenced by Nono and the scores he left in Poland.

It can probably be said with some authority that this early period of isolation, caused by the political situation in Poland in the post-World War II period, allowed Penderecki the opportunity to formulate his own original compositional style. Those Western European influences he encountered at the end of these student years modified his own expression rather than restricting it. He was now ready to embark on his own career as a composer.

Early Professional Life

Penderecki's early professional life consisted primarily of teaching and composing. Most of the time was spent in Poland because he had neither the financial means nor the political influence to travel outside the country. His high marks at the Academy and the success of the "Epitaph" earned him an immediate appointment to the faculty of his Alma Mater. To earn extra money he also lectured at the Krakow Theological Seminary and served as a correspondent for the periodical, *Ruch Muzyczny*, in which he wrote - not as a critic, but as a journalist - a column entitled "Performance of New Works". He also wrote music for the puppet theater in Krakow.

Most of the works of these early post-student years were not written in a cloistered study but in the busy environment of *Jama Michalika*, a coffee house in the heart of the old city of Krakow. At a small table in the corner of the room, the young composer sat day after day, not just every morning at breakfast, but also at other times when he felt like composing. The atmosphere on a quiet afternoon especially animated him. His first wife, Barbara, a pianist, practiced at home in their tiny apartment while their daughter slept. They had married very young (1954) while Penderecki was still a student at the Academy. In these circumstances Penderecki found the coffee house conducive to work and creativity.[10]

These early years in Krakow were filled not just with composing and teaching, but also with trips to other cities within Poland. He visited Warsaw and Danzig and wrote music for the theaters there. Often he travelled to Lodż where he composed music to short films and children's films.

The first of the post-student compositions to receive a performance in Krakow was the *Psalms of David* (1958), a ten-minute piece for mixed chorus and orchestra at Philharmonic Hall on October 9, 1959. At its first performance, the critics noted an affinity with Stravinsky's *Symphony of Psalms* (1948) and some of the early works of Carl Orff. His next works were *Emanations* (1958), for two string orchestras, and *Strophes* (1959), for soprano, speaker and ten instruments.

On the basis of these early efforts, Penderecki was encouraged to enter anonymously these three works in a competition sponsored by the Polish Composers Association. Its purpose was to encourage the young composers of the country. Established one year earlier, it was the most important event of its type in Poland for young composers and included among the members of the jury such famous Polish composers and teachers as Witold Lutoslawski, Kazimierz Sikorski and Stanislaw Wiechowicz. After the judging was completed and the members of the panel opened the envelopes which contained the names of the three prize-winning works, they were amazed to discover that they had given the first three awards to the young Krakow Academy professor, Krzysztof Penderecki. *Strophes* was awarded first prize, while *Emanations* and the *Psalms of David* were both given the second prize. This was a triumph without parallel and immediately placed the twenty-five year old composer in a position of leadership among the Polish avant-gardists.

Many of the characteristics that were to become typical of Penderecki's compositional style in this period of exploration (1958-1962) were adumbrated in *Strophes*, including unconventional notation, free progression unhindered by normal meter and tempo, partially-controlled aleatory structures, and experimentation with both vocal and instrumental sonorities. The unusual text of this work combined the writings of Menander, Sophocles, Isaiah, Jeremiah and Omar Khayyam and demonstrated to the jury that here was a composer who not only produced musical sounds in an unusual manner but who also was well-read and possessed a feeling for language. Another characteristic of these compositions, and one clearly evident in *Strophes*, was a certain kind of experimentation with twelve-tone technique. Although he eventually abandoned the twelve-tone method as too confining for his needs, its use in these early works in a limited way[11] is significant. Speaking of this early use of serialism and his subsequent rejection of it as a compositional idiom, he revealed in an interview in *The New York Times* that the compositional style which he eventually developed was "a direct reaction against the Webern style as practiced and promulgated at Darmstadt" (the Darmstadt summer festival of contemporary music).[12]

In addition to the prize for the Warsaw competition, there was a scholarship for a two-month study trip to Italy that began in December, 1959. On this journey, his first outside Poland to a Western European country, he visited some of the important cities of Italy - Venice, Florence, Rome, Naples, and even Sicily - and also re-newed his friendship with the composer Luigi Nono, who was living in Florence at the time. The journey was a broadening experience for Penderecki and provided additional impetus to his desire to explore new musical horizons.

The years 1959 and 1960 were a time of intense experimentation for the young composer. Following the success of the Warsaw competition and the premiere of the *Psalms of David*, Penderecki completed no less than six works during this two year period.[13] Just prior to his Italian trip he finished the *Miniatures for Violin and Piano* (1959), a short three-movement work which represented his first attempt at maintaining a non-metric scheme throughout an entire composition. The *Miniatures* also exhibit some of the characteristics of the *Three Pieces for Violoncello and*

Piano of Anton Webern (1881-1943), especially in their brevity and their use of free atonality.

But here the similarity ends, for it is the use of tone colors and the experiments with string sounds that captures the attention of the listener in the Penderecki work, thus foreshadowing what was to become a dominant characteristic of all his works through the first two periods of his compositional style (1958-1962; 1962-1974), and indeed of the entire Polish avant-garde during the decade of the 1960s. This aspect of Polish music was described rather succinctly in the European periodical *Melos*: "Innovations in the West were primarily directed against something, against false compromises with the past, against the force of a once more flourishing and self-pleasing objectivity. The modern music of Poland raised its voice *for* (italics ours) something: for a certain life feeling (to which the music owed its existence), for a concept of freedom and individual responsibility which was until then almost unknown, and which stamped the music with a special character. Its sphere of activity was even greater and the radius of its possibilities was less constricted."[14]

Penderecki continued his experiments with serialism, unconventional time systems, unusual instrumental sonorities and extended vocal-choral techniques in such works as *Anaklasis* (1960) for 42 strings and percussion and *Dimensions of Time and Silence* (1960) for mixed chorus, string instruments and percussion. *Anaklasis* brought the composer his first international recognition since it was the first of his works to receive its premiere performance in a Western European country. Composed for the Donaueschingen Festival in the Black Forest of Southern Germany, it created quite a stir at its first performance on October 22, 1960: "*Anaklasis* provided the excuse for the only near-riot of the Festival," wrote Everett Helm. "Incorporating quarter-tones, glissandi, and many other highly unusual (*recherché*) devices, it maintained a tension of a rather frightening sort throughout. In response to the boss and whistling (Hans) Rosbaud repeated the work."[15]

Wolfram Schwinger, writing some years later, viewed *Anaklasis* in a broader perspective as a work in which Penderecki showed himself already in 1960 as a natural master of the new area of composition he was exploring, "one with which he influenced a whole movement in composition - *Farbenmusik* (literally, color music), the borderline between sound and noise, where new techniques of playing were developed . . . and where a completely new notation, based on graphic elements, was now used by many composers."[16]

If *Anaklasis* was Penderecki's first real experimental work for orchestra, *Dimensions* demonstrated how far-reaching his exploration of vocal colors could extend. As the only work of his to receive its world premiere at the Warsaw Autumn Festival (September 18, 1960), this fourteen-minute composition uses the chorus as a percussion section and provides an introduction to some of the vocal techniques later found in the *St. Luke Passion* (movement 10, pages 33-42). No words are sung here, only harshly-produced slavic consonant sounds (z ż sz cż) which are arranged serially. The *Musical America* review of the first performance described *Dimensions* as "varicolored lines and structures . . . joined by means of permeation; the mixed chorus . . . takes over the function of percussion and also serves to produce rustling effects by an appropriate combination of whistling and sibilants."[17]

The importance of the Warsaw Autumn Festival in launching Penderecki's career and bringing his music to the attention of composers and critics outside Poland cannot be overestimated. When the first festival was held in 1957, and the earliest Polish pointillist twelve-tone works were produced, it was not long before outsiders began to talk of Poland as the musical phoenix of Eastern Europe. The festival lasted for nine days, each of which was packed with exciting events that included two (sometimes three) concerts. New works of Polish composers were recorded and issued two or three days after they were performed. Musical connoisseurs from around the world took the news of these events back to their respective countries. The Warsaw Autumn Festival thus became the showcase from which Penderecki would emerge as one of the leading figures of contemporary music. The success of the *St. Luke Passion* in 1966 gave credibility to these early indications of an original and special talent. *Dimensions of Time and Silence* received its world premiere in 1960; *Threnody* was performed at the festival one year later.

Threnody for the Victims of Hiroshima (1960) was the first of five compositions written between 1960 and 1962 in which Penderecki sought to derive new and unusual sounds from traditional stringed instruments. This work gained almost instant international acclaim after its Warsaw premiere on May 31, 1961. The title caught the imagination of listeners and music critics alike; the musical public sensed immediately an aural association between the dense sonorities of massed 52-part strings and the horror of the nuclear explosion that occurred over that unfortunate Japanese city in 1945. What made the reaction of the audience all the more interesting was Penderecki's claim that he had originally conceived this work as an abstract piece of music entitled "Eight minutes and thirty-seven seconds;" the dedication to the victims of Hiroshima was added after the work was completed. The dense clusters which gave the work its distinctive sound were used a great deal in later works, expecially in the *St. Luke Passion*.

Soon after the second performance of *Threnody*, at the 1961 Warsaw Autumn Festival, the *New York Times* referred to Penderecki as the "*enfant terrible* of Polish Music", and pointed out that he had dispensed with the "concept of exact pitch and intervals as an organizing factor in composition - thus with anything resembling melodic or harmonic relationships."[18] Nevertheless, *Threnody* earned the composer a UNESCO award, as well as the Fitelberg Prize, the Polish Ministry of Culture Award (Polish State Artistic Prize), and recognition by the *Tribune Internationale des Compositeurs* in Paris.

The year 1960 marked Penderecki's second extended stay in Western Europe. As a result of his trip to the Donaueschingen Festival in the fall to attend the premiere of *Anaklasis* (October 22, 1960), he was invited to live in Celle (West Germany) during the fall months in the home of the publisher Hermann Moeck.[19] It is thus not surprising that Moeck Verlag was the first publishing firm in the West to distribute his music. This year also marked the completion of his *String Quartet No. 1*, a work which would be the first of his compositions to receive a first performance in the United States.[20]

Penderecki's continued exploration of the range of possibilities for stringed instruments saw the conception and completion in 1961 of one of his most interesting works. His fascination with the unorthodox led him to record the brainwaves of a number of mental patients (at the Krakow Medical Center, where he was working as a volunteer) as they listened to a tape recording of *Threnody*.

The resultant encephalographs were used as the basis of the glissando-like melodic material in *Polymorphia* (1961), a work for 48 strings which received its first performance in April, 1962 in Hamburg (West Germany) by the North German Radio Orchestra, under the direction of Andrzej Markowski.

These experiments with pure sound and instrumental sonorities reached their extreme with two works which were composed in 1962: *Kanon*, for string orchestra and two tape recorders, and a piece for orchestra entitled *Fluorescences*. Scored for an extremely large orchestra and a percussion battery that included a metal plate and a saw, the work, at the Donaueschingen premiere, moved one critic to write: "All that was left was sawdust . . . and an unfavorable impression!"[21]

It was apparent by 1962 that Penderecki's experiments with instruments had been taken to an extreme. Even the composer recognized that he was at an important crossroad: "The solution to my dilemma," he stated at an interview some years later, "was not to go forward and perhaps destroy the spirit of music as a result, but to gain inspiration from the past and to look back on my heritage."[22] The clear style of *Stabat Mater* (1962) was the immediate result of this return to tradition, the road to a personal style that would lead eventually to the *St. Luke Passion* (1965-1966).

Stabat Mater and the Evolution of the Passion

Stabat Mater, written for three a cappella mixed choruses, marked an important change in direction for Penderecki and paved the way for the *Passion* into which it was incorporated in its entirety three years later. It is evident from the sketches which were made as early as October 1959 that this new style had been evolving in his thoughts for some time. But it was not until the summer of 1962 that the work began to take shape; it was finished in August of that year while the composer was vacationing in Jurata, a small village on the Polish Baltic Sea. Its completion marked the beginning of a new period in his works, a period of stability that characterized his compositional output between the years 1962 and 1974.

The musical significance of *Stabat Mater* was that it integrated the new tone colors and textures which Penderecki had developed in his period of exploration (1958-1962) into a meaningful relationship with the traditional elements of pitch, rhythm and form. The chant-like rondo theme that unified the work formally was diatonic in structure and rhythmically constant. The tone clusters used in *Stabat Mater* were written in such a way that they "fan out" from a unison tonal center; this made their performance easier for a vocal ensemble. The work received its first performance on November 27, 1962 by the Polish Radio Chorus in Warsaw.

The success of *Stabat Mater* and the new style which it established brought the composer new and broader recognition as a serious creator of the New Music. The momentum toward the composition of choral works that it generated was not to slacken until 1974 when he began work on the opera *Paradise Lost*. This was a period during which Penderecki produced his most important works for this performing medium. The *Cantata* (*In Honorem Alma Matris Iagellonae*), written for the 600th Anniversary of the University of Krakow, was completed in the spring of 1964. *St. Luke* followed in 1965, and *Dies Irae* (1967), for the victims of Auschwitz, two years later. The large two-part work *Utrenia*, based on the traditional Eastern Orthodox liturgy, was composed in 1967 (Part I) and 1968 (Part II). *Kosmogonia*, the result of a commission for the 25th Anniversary of the United Nations, followed in 1970. *Ecloga* VIII (1972) and *Canticum Canticorum Salomonis* (1972-1973), perhaps his most experimental choral work, came next; and this second style period was rounded out by *Magnificat* (1973-1974), commissioned by the Salzburg Festival. During these years he also composed fourteen instrumental works.

The commission to write the *St. Luke Passion* came in the fall of 1962.[23] It was the result of his success at the Donaueschingen Festival and his association with Dr. Otto Tomek, the director of the department of new music at the West German Radio in Cologne. For some time Penderecki had been thinking of writing a large work for orchestra and chorus on the theme of the Passion. This idea, and the plan of the West German Radio to commission a work for the celebration of the founding of the Cathedral at Münster, came together in discussions with Dr. Tomek during the summer of 1962, when the composer was in Donaueschingen for the premiere of *Fluorescences*. The arrangements were finalized at the Warsaw Autumn Festival in the fall of the same year.

The first section of the work to be completed after *Stabat Mater* was the soprano aria (No. 4) written initially in 1964 as an orchestra piece, "Lamento" on the death of Bronislaw Rutkowski, the Rector of the Krakow Academy of Music. Two other works were completed in 1964, thereby interrupting again the progress on *St. Luke*. The *Cantata* (1964) received its first performance on May 10 in Krakow, and the *Sonata for Violoncello and Orchestra*, written for Siegfried Palm and the Southwest German Radio Orchestra, was premiered on October 18, 1964 at the Donaueschingen Festival.

Next came the Passacaglia (No. 16), the great *homage* to J. S. Bach, which was composed in December 1964 and January 1965. The work on St. Luke was interrupted, however, by his other compositional activities, including a commission from the Polish Radio to write a radio score for Bohdan Drozdowski's *Todesbridage* (Death Brigade). This electronic work, one of the very few the composer wrote for this compositional medium, was one of the most dramatic and original scores produced by the Polish Radio.

The year 1965 found the composer living in Krakow and working on the three a cappella Passion movements and the *Capriccio for Oboe* (1965), which had been commissioned by the Lucerne (Switzerland) Festival. "Te fons salutis," "Miserere" (No. 12) and "In Pulverem Mortis" (No. 20) were written in April and May. Penderecki went to Cologne in April to meet with Dr. Tomek and begin the process of gathering the instrumental and vocal resources for the premiere. The trip to Germany provided the motivation which led subsequently to the completion of the opening movement (No. 1) on June 14.

The most important event of the year, which occurred right in the midst of the feverish work on St. Luke, was Penderecki's marriage to Elizabeth Solecka, a student at the University of Krakow and the daughter of the principal cellist of the Krakow Philharmonic Orchestra. Following their wedding on June 18, the Pendereckis traveled to Switzerland where the *Cappricio for Oboe* received its first performance at the Lucerne Festival.

The solo parts and the remainder of the work were completed during a six week period beginning December 9, 1955. The Passion was finished on

"26 January 1966", a little over two months before the premiere, and dedicated to his young wife, Elizabeth.[24]

The Premiere

The world premiere of St. Luke took place on the Wednesday evening of Holy Week (March 30, 1966) in keeping with the liturgical tradition that the 22nd and 23rd chapters of the Gospel of Luke were to be read on this day. Its importance as a musical event was underscored by the fact that more than 50 German and 15 foreign reporters attended. It is interesting to note that while music critics were present from Poland, Holland, France, Sweden, Switzerland, and, of course, Germany, there were no representatives present from the English speaking countries.[25]

On the morning of the concert, a press conference was held by the West German Radio in the City Hall in Münster. It was at this time that Penderecki discussed his thoughts about the Passion and gave his reasons for the selection of the St. Luke text. He also explained in some detail the influence of J. S. Bach on this work and the underlying meaning of the Passion text in the twentieth century:

> The Passion is the suffering and death of Christ, but it is also the suffering and death at Auschwitz, the tragic experience of mankind, in the middle of the twentieth century. In this sense, it should according to my intentions and feelings have a universal, humanistic character like Threnody.[13]

In attendance at the premiere was the personal representative of Pope Paul VI, the Apostolic Nuncio Archbishop C. Bafile, the highest church official in West Germany. The ceremonial nature of the event was heightened by the entrance of the Archbishop Bafile, Bishop Dr. Joseph Höffner, the ranking prelate in Münster, the Cathedral Chapter, and the Clergy of the City, all dressed in their festive regalia.[27]

These special guests, the officials of the City of Münster, the staff of the West German Radio, and the more than 1,000 others who filled the Cathedral that evening could hardly have been prepared for the new sounds they were about to hear, much less realize that they were participating in an event of great historical importance. However, according to the report of Wolfram Schwinger, "one could read strong emotions on many of the faces, a strong emotion that was appropriate to a contemporary work on the timeless theme of the Passion."[28]

The performance itself, which began at 8:00 p.m. and was broadcast simultaneously over the West German Radio, included four of the composer's fellow Poles in featured roles: the conductor, Henryk Czyż, musical director of the Krakow Philharmonic; and the soloists, Stefania Woytowicz (soprano), Andrzej Hiolski (baritone), in the role of Jesus, and Bernard Ladysz (bass). The Evangelist, a spoken part, was narrated by Rudolf Jürgen Bartsch. The other performers included the Tölzer Boy's Choir and the Cologne Radio Chorus and Symphony Orchestra.

17

Following the concert there was a reception in the Great Hall of the Collegium Borromäum. Among the many speeches that usually accompany an event of this type in Germany, the words of Klaus von Bismarck, the director of the West German Radio, were especially poignant in that they referred to the necessary reconciliation between Germany and Poland. It was he who said, "Music at all times has shown itself to be a good bridge over the streams that divide us politically."[29]

In the many performances which took place in the period immediately following the Münster premiere, the words of von Bismarck proved to be prophetic indeed; the timeless theme of the *Passion* and the originality of Penderecki's musical language were able to transcend the cultural and ideological barriers that separate people in the late twentieth century.

Reactions to the Premiere

The critical acclaim that accompanied the premiere surprised even the most enthusiastic of Penderecki's supporters. Heinz Josef Herbort, writing in the prestigious *Die Zeit*, set the tone for the many reviews which followed the concert:

> People will count Penderecki's Passion Music as among the most important compositions within the new music. The clarity of the revolutionary score, the logic of the construction of the work, and the penetrating effect from the music is far superior to the choral music written even by prominent composers in recent years.[30]

Hans Heinz Stuckenschmidt, well known as a specialist in twentieth century music, covered the premiere for the German periodical *Melos*. His review added further credibility to the success of the Passion:

> After Webern's religious choral works and Stravinsky's late works, Penderecki with his Passion music has built the most important bridge between the liturgical spirit and the new music.[31]

The critic for *Die Welt*, Hanspeter Krellmann, wrote about the eclectic nature of Penderecki's compositional style:

> Krzysztof Penderecki is not only one of the most gifted composers in Poland, he may also be one of the strongest personalities of the New Music. He has no school of composition. He does not know any doctrines, nor any simple way. He uses every possibility of sound from the dry linearity of Stravinsky through the dodecaphonists and up to Stockhausen's subjective extrovertism. Everything he develops and proves. From all these styles, he selects in a free way. He melts his own style with those of others.[32]

Awards Received for St. Luke

With the completion of the *St. Luke Passion*, the list of Penderecki's works now numbered twenty. But it was this one work alone which was to insure the composer's international fame and his special place in the history of twentieth-century music. In recognition of the work, the West German State of North Rhine-Westphalia conferred upon Penderecki its Grand Prize for 1966. The same year he received Poland's Peace Prize, as well as the Jurzyskowski Prize of the Polish Institute of Arts and Sciences. In 1967, the composer received the "Prix Italie" of the Italian Radio (RAI).

Subsequent Performances

Following shortly upon the successful premiere, other performances of St. Luke were soon given in Poland and Italy. Within twenty-four months of the first performance, the work had been heard in Krakow, Wroclaw, Venice, Warsaw, Turin, Belgrade, London, Amsterdam, Rotterdam, Dubrovnik, Minneapolis, Stuttgart, Paris, Stockholm, Berlin and Rome. If there was ever any doubt after the success of the Münster premiere, these subsequent performances firmly established St. Luke as one of the most important works of the time and assured the international fame of the composer.

Twenty-three days after the work was heard in Germany, the first Polish performance was given in the composer's adopted home town. Scheduled appropriately on April 22 (St. Luke's Day) in Philharmonic Hall, this second performance featured the three soloists who had appeared in the premiere. This Krakow premiere also featured a new narrator, Leszek Herdegen, who was joined by the Boy's Chorus, Mixed Chorus and Orchestra of the Krakow Philharmonic. The conductor was Henryk Czyż.[33]

The Münster performance was recorded for RCA Victrola, and the Krakow performance was recorded for Philips within the same month. It is doubtful if any other twentieth century work has enjoyed such instantaneous recognition by the classical recording industry.

Nine other readings of St. Luke took place in Penderecki's native Poland during the work's first six months. The performance in Krakow's Wawel Castle in June attracted an audience of 15,000, according to the report in the German periodical *Polen*.[34] Such a turnout, in a country where public attendance at religious events outside the church was forbidden, demonstrated the vitality of Christianity in that country and confirmed the power of the Passion to speak to people in a variety of circumstances. The Wawel concert also proved the appeal of the *Passion* as a religious statement for the people of Poland.

> It could well be said that such a work as this could only have been written by someone whose whole life had been spent within the Roman communion, by someone who knows and accepts quite naturally every inflection of the Roman liturgy and the religious truth which is embodied within it. It possesses, too, something of the absolute conviction of a people who, for ten often very turbulent centuries, have found hope and consolation in their unshakable faith.[35]

19

On September 24th, the work was heard for the first time at the prestigious Warsaw Autumn Festival. This performance, which marked the fourth time that one of the composer's works had received a hearing at the Festival, was viewed by those who had attended these concerts on a regular basis as a kind of summary statement of his development as a composer between the years 1959 and 1966. Writing on the occasion of the Warsaw performance, the critic of the *Musical Times* stated:

> It was a tremendous occasion; Poland after all is a deeply Catholic country. Those who knew only Penderecki's *Hiroshima (Threnody)* with its extraordinary effects for strings may have doubted whether he could bring off such a formidable task in our time as a Passion; but the performance under Henryk Czyż left no doubt as to its remarkable qualities.[36]

In between these Polish performances, the group from the West German Radio which had given the premiere in Münster, was heard on September 14 in the Italian premiere at the XXIXth Biennale Festival in Venice. Sharing the limelight with the Russian pianist Sviatoslav Richter and the premiere of Luigi Nono's opera, *Intolerance 1960*, the performance of the *Passion* closed the Festival and provided the music critics present the opportunity to comment on the contrasting musical and political aspects of these two new works. Nono's electronic score was based on a text which included the writings of Castro, Kahn, Lumumba and anonymous critics of the Vietnam War, texts from the point of view of the left which provided a contrast to the message of the Passion.[37]

After the spectacular reports that had followed the performances in Germany and Poland, the British premiere on May 24, 1967 at London's Festival was awaited with much anticipation by the press:

> The *St. Luke Passion* is Penderecki's most ambitious and highly acclaimed work, bringing to fruition all the various expressive ideas and technical procedures which he explored so thoroughly in earlier works. When it was heard for the first time it won the immediate acclaim of the Church, of musicians and the public alike. And the powerful impact it made on that occasion has been repeated at each performance. Clearly, then, a work such as this, which has been described as one of the most important contributions to the religious music of our time, and which has made so deep an impression on so many people, should be heard not just once, but many times, for only when its language has become thoroughly familiar will it fully reveal its true essence.[38]

There were two London performances, one at Festival Hall and the other at Royal Albert Hall. The three soloists - Stefania Woytowicz, Bernard Ladysz and Andrezj Hiolski - and the conductor, Henryk Czyż, were brought to London for the premiere, while the other participants included the BBC Orchestra, Chorus and Choral Society, the choir of the Ealing Grammar School and Narrator, John Westbrook.

With the extremely dry acoustics of Festival Hall complicating the problem, the first London performance was anything but a critical success. Robert Henderson, writing in the July issue of the *Musical Times*, expressed the disappointment of those who attended the premiere:

Some doubts were also cast on the actual success of Penderecki's attempt to renew the tradition of the Bach Passions in contemporary terms to construct a large-scale work which, while using uncompromisingly avant-garde techniques, would yet speak directly to the public-at-large. In listening to the record many times over several weeks, I had been impressed above all by the work's deeply moving, liturgical flavour, by the intensity of the composer's response to the quality of the words which seemed to bind together the multifarious and often astonishingly novel effects into a coherent, infinitely moving design. In the concert hall, however, some of these effects began to sound suspiciously modish, the music in general being never quite so compelling, nor appearing quite so finely integrated. Only time, and many more performances, will disclose which of these reactions was the correct one.[39]

The editorial comment which appeared in the same periodical following the second English performance in Royal Albert Hall elicited a completely different and much more positive response:

Nor was it just a question of the Promenaders' unbounded enthusiasm; as the music filled the hall, one could feel the audience being drawn into the experience, becoming involved, becoming profoundly moved.[40]

This introduction of the *Passion* to the English-speaking world was followed a little over four months later by the American premiere on November 2, 1967 in Minneapolis, Minnesota. Conducted by a fellow Pole, Stanislaw Skrowaczewski, who was at the time the musical director of the Minneapolis Symphony (now Minnesota Orchestra), the soloists included Dorothy Dorow, the soprano who had sung in the Warsaw Autumn Festival performance; Andrzej Hiolski, the baritone who had sung the part of Jesus in the Münster world premiere; and bass Arnold Voketaitis. The actor Lee Richardson spoke the narrative of the Evangelist. The Minneapolis Symphony was joined by the Choirs of Macalester College and the Boy's Choir of St. Paul's Cathedral.

The same group of performers also gave the first New York performance on March 6, 1969, a reading that was postponed sixteen months due to the illness of Skrowaczewski. In the words of Alan Rich, writing in *New York Magazine*,

"All the Right People were there - Copland, Carter, Cage, Sessions, Babbitt, Feldman - at a concert of new music. The reception at the end was powerful and prolonged, the cheers finally winning out over the boos. This, despite the work's challenge, its prevailingly somber atmosphere, and the fact that Penderecki had as yet written no movie scores nor appeared on the Carson show. His reputation has, in fact, come entirely from his music and not vice versa."[42]

This Carnegie Hall event, which drew a capacity audience, was covered by most of the important East Coast critics. It was an unusual succes for Penderecki in New York, where he has always been viewed by the press with some skepticism. Three excerpts from the many reviews of the concert will suffice:

21

The St. Luke Passion has undeniable effectiveness, and it strongly emphasizes the text . . . There is no denying the modernism of the score, and yet it does not sound modern. Can this be one of those pieces of modern music for people who hate modern music?[43]

Harold C. Schonberg
New York Times

It is the work of an objective contemporary mind reinterpreting an ancient legend, and in this respect, Penderecki's ninety-minute Passion is never less than a fascinating and intense work of an expert craftsman. Why this work has made Penderecki an international celebrity in the past three years was made clear by the simple fact that his style, eclectic as it may be, communicates.[44]

Robert Jacobson
Saturday Review

The *Passion* is an extraordinary piece, powerful, genuinely moving, able to engage both mind and gut. At a time when non-involvement is often prized, it is an extremely involved piece . . . I had predicted months ago that this would be the most distinguished event of the season, and I retract nothing.[45]

Alan Rich
New York Magazine

One of the more unusual performances of the *Passion* took place in Düsseldorf, West Germany, twenty-three days after the New York premiere. With the full consent of the composer, the *Deutsche Oper am Rhein* presented a fully-staged version of the work. Following in its tradition of scenic performances of large choral works (previous productions had included Monteverdi's *Orfeo* and *Combattimento*, Dallapiccola's *Job*, and Schönberg's *Moses and Aaron*), the Düsseldorf Opera engaged Henryk Czyż, Stefania Woytowicz, and Rudolf Jürgen Bartsch from the original cast. The other performers, including orchestra and chorus, were selected from the resident company.[46]

Because of negative reviews the production received as a result of its initial performance on March 29, 1969, Penderecki undoubtedly regretted that he had given his permission for the staged version. It was not only criticized as a theatrical event, the musical impression was dimmed as well. The rather explicit review in *Opera News* tells the entire story:

In spite of this big investment, the Düsseldorf premiere left one seriously disillusioned - not only about the theatrical validity of the work but, worse, about its musical merits. The set was a diagonally raised ampitheatre for the chorus, which appeared in civilian clothes, and a bare center stage for the action of Christ and His Cross. There were two cycloramas, one white and the other black, and numerous projections - now objective, strongly symbolic, and, finally, commonplace. At its best this staging was merely superfluous. At its worst, mostly in the big chorus scenes and orchestral interludes, it mercilessly exposed the purely illustrative tendency of the music.[47]

In spite of the bad press, one more dramatic production was given in Hannover (1969).[48]

Performances of the Passion followed in most of the major cities of the world and, by the work's tenth anniversary in 1976, well over one hundred had been given. American readings occurred, in addition to those discussed above, in Minneapolis and New York, in San Francisco (1969), Pittsburgh (1969), Nashville (1969), Dallas (1970), Atlanta (1970), Los Angeles (Chapman College, 1971), Washington, D.C. (1973), Cincinnati (1973), Tacoma (1974), and Cleveland (1980).[49]

Clearly, the St. Luke Passion was now established as one of the major works of twentieth century sacred choral literature; in retrospect it is also clear that it was among a group of works that signalled a significant style change in contemporary music. For decades composers had been pushing music in two extreme directions - toward the extreme control of total serialism and towards the extreme freedom of aleatory composition and *Farbenmusik*. Though evidences of these trends are still present in some sections of the *St. Luke Passion*, they are used more for expressive than for experimental purposes. Other parts represent a return to such traditional characteristics as melodic lyricism, contrapuntal elaboration and tonal centricity, not in a neo-Classic, neo-Baroque, or neo-Romantic sense, but in the sense of an highly personal continuation of the core of musical tradition. Its place in music history was perhaps best summarized by Harold Schonberg, music critic for *The New York Times*, in his editorial following the Carnegie Hall performance:

What the "Saint Luke" Passion does offer, and what the Carnegie Hall audience responded to (the performance was a smash succes), is an aesthetic re-orientation that may be very significant. The score is a complete breakaway from the type of post-Webern writing practiced by such exponents as Stockhausen, Xenakis and many of the Americans. Whether or not "Saint Luke" lives as a viable piece of music, it does illustrate a movement that tries to take music out of abstractionism into something that has a direct contact with life and reality. It may be one of those transitional scores res that lead the way toward a new approach. In this case the approach is away from the complexity of the post-serialists into something infinitely more direct.[50]

Notes

Chapter I

1 Wolfgang Bürde, "Berlin" Alban Berg's 'Lulu' - Krzysztof Penderecki's 'Lukas-Passion,' *Neue Zeitschrift für Musik* 139 (April 1968), p. 185.

2 While there have been other Passion settings for chorus and orchestra since Beethoven, notably *Des Heilands letze Stunden* (1835) of Louis Spohr (1784-1859), the Penderecki *St. Luke Passion* is the first work in this form to approach the greatness of the Bach Passions.

3 Heinz Josef Herbort, "Belehrung aus Polen," *Die Zeit*, 4 April 1966, p. 20.

4 Hans Heinz Stuckenschmidt, "Polnische Passion in Dom zu Münster," *Melos* 33 (May 1966), p. 152.

5 The city of Dębica is located about 150 miles east of Krakow and approximately the same distance west of the Russian border.

6 *Newsweek*, 17 March 1969.

7 Harold Patton, "Penderecki, Composer of the Last Judgement," *Chicagoland and FM Guide* (April 1968), p. 37.

8 Antes Orga, "Penderecki: Composer of Martyrdom," *Music and Musicians* 18 (September 1969), p. 34.

9 Luigi Nono was a confirmed Communist who desired to have his music performed before the Polish workers. Their less than enthusiastic response to this avant-garde music was a source of considerable disillusionment to him. Interview with Krzysztof Penderecki, Krakow, Poland, 17 August 1977.

10 Penderecki claims that all or part of six works were written in this coffee house: *Anaklasis*, *Threnody*, *Dimensions of Time and Silence*, *String Quartet No. 1*, *Polymorphia* and *Fluorescences*.

11 Penderecki's use of serial technique has always been limited. On occasion, it has been employed in the classic Schönbergian manner as, for example, in the second movement of the *Psalms of David* (1958); but usually it is used at the composer's convenience. The basic rules of twelve-tone technique are rarely observed.

12 *New York Times* (22 February 1969): Sec. 2, p. 19.

13 *Strophes* (1959), *Miniatures for Violin and Piano* (1959), *Anaklasis* (1959-1960), *Dimensions of Time and Silence* (1959-1960), *Threnody* (1960), and *String Quartet No. 1* (1960) were all completed during this period.

14 Ulrich Debelius, "Polish Avant-Garde," *Melos* 37 (1956): p. 4.

15 Everett Helm, "Donaueschingen - 1960," *Musical Times* 101 (December 1960): p. 772.

16 Wolfgang Schwinger, "Penderecki and 'The Devils,'" *Opera* 24 (November 1973): p. 961.

17 Ernst Thomas, "ISCM Meeting," *Musical America LXXXI*, September 1961, p. 2.

18 Everett Helm, "Nine Day Festival," *New York Times* (8 October 1961): Sec. 2, p. 13.

19 Interview with Krzysztof Penderecki, Krakow, Poland, 14 August 1977.

20 The *String Quartet No. 1* was premiered on 11 May 1962 in Cincinnati, Ohio by the La Salle String Quartet. The contact with this ensemble was made by the publisher Hermann Moeck.

21 "Fünf Stimmen über Donaueschingen 1962", *Melos* 29 (December 1962): p. 397.

22 Antes Orga, "Krzysztof Penderecki," *Music and Musicians* 22 (October 1973): p. 39.

23 "Im Auftrag des WDR: Die Lukas-Passion von Penderecki," *Kirche und Rundfunk* (Köln), 6 April 1966.

24 The score of the *St. Luke Passion* (Moeck Verlag, 1968) included the completion date and the dedication to Elizabeth.

25 "Passion in Neuer Klangwelt aus dem Geist unserer Zeit," *Siegener Zeitung*, 6 April 1966.

26 Ryszard Wasita, "Avantgarde und Erbe," *Polen*, July 1966. Interview with Krzysztof Penderecki at the time of the premiere of the *St. Luke Passion*. Münster, FRG.

27 Hanspeter Krellmann, "Passion aus Polen," *Die Welt*, 4 April 1966.

28 Wolfram Schwinger, *Penderecki: Begegnungen, Lebensdaten, Werkkommentare* (Stuttgart: Deutsche Verlagsanstalt, 1979), p. 45.

29 Karl Kurt Ziegler, "Lukas-Passion in Neuer Klangwelt," *Westfälische Rundschau*, 1 April 1966.

30 Heinz Josef Herbort, "Belehrung aus Polen," *Die Zeit*, 8 April 1966.

31 Hans Heinz Stuckenschmidt, "Polnische Passion," *Frankfurter Allgemeine Zeitung*, 6 April 1966.

32 Hanspeter Krellmann, "Passion aus Polen," *Die Welt*, April 4, 1966.

33 Archives of Moeck Verlag, Celle, West Germany.

34 "Genutzte Chance," *Polen*, September 9, 1966.

35 Robert Henderson, "Penderecki's St. Luke Passion," *Musical Times* CVII (May 1967), p. 423.

36 Frederick Page, "Warsaw - Penderecki's Passion," *Musical Times* 107 (December 1966), p. 1079.

37 "Jahrmarkt der Novitäten," *Wiesbadener Kurier*, 13 September 1966.

38 Robert Henderson, "Penderecki's 'St. Luke Passion,'" *Musical Times* 108 (July 1967), p. 422.

39 Robert Henderson, "Penderecki," *Musical Times* 108 (July 1967), p. 624.

40 Stanley Sadie, "Editorial," *Musical Times* 108 (September 1967), p. 793.

41 *Minneapolis Symphony Concert Program*, November 1967.

42 Alan Rich, "The Music Critic as Sex Symbol," *New York Magazine* (31 March 1969).

43 Harold C. Schonberg, "Romanticism Coming Up?," *New York Times*, 16 March 1969).

44 Robert Jacobson, "Penderecki's Passion," *Saturday Review* (22 March 1969).

45 Alan Rich, *New York Magazine*, 16 March 1969.

46 Heinrich von Lüttwitz, "Barfuss hat langfristige Pläne," *Rheinische Post*, 4 April 1967.

47 Horst Koegler, "Düsseldorf," *Opera News* (14 June 1969), p. 25.

48 Archive of Moeck Verlag, Celle, West Germany

49 Ibid.

50 Harold C. Schonberg, *New York Times*, 16 March 1969.

Chapter II

A BRIEF HISTORY OF THE PASSION

The Passion story, in any of its four renderings in the Gospels, is filled with dramatic content. Because of its association with the most solemn season of the liturgical year, it has received the attention of the leading composers from the time its musical setting was first accepted by the liturgical authorities. It is significant that Penderecki, a composer who has specialized in the large dramatic musical form, would choose the Passion text for his first large choral work. By this decision he joined a long line of important composers who have produced some of their finest works while under the inspiration of this text, notably Antoine de Longueval, Gilles de Binchois, Johann Walter, Tomás Luis de Victoria, Orlando di Lasso, Leonhard Lechner, Heinrich Schütz, J.S. Bach, Georg Philipp Telemann, Franz Joseph Haydn, Ludwig van Beethoven, Hugo Distler and Ernst Pepping. The purpose of this chapter is to survey some of the highlights in the historical development of the Passion as a musical form. This short history will begin with the early settings of Passion story.

Early settings of the Passion story

In early times the Passion text was simply read during Holy Week. The earliest record of a Passion reading in a religious ceremony is described by the pilgrim Egeria who wrote about the Holy Week services he observed during a visit to Jerusalem in the fourth century A.D. In the middle of the fifth century, Pope Leo the Great decreed that the St. Matthew account should be read during the Mass for Palm Sunday and the Wednesday in Holy Week, while that of St. John should be included in the Good Friday liturgy. The passage in St. Luke eventually replaced St. Matthew as the Wednesday reading in the seventh century. In the tenth century, if became the practice to read the St. Mark Passion account on Tuesday. Thus the Holy Week recitations of the Passion story in Latin were established as follows: Palm Sunday, St. Matthew, Chapters 26 and 27; Tuesday, St. Mark, Chapters 14 und 15; Wednesday, St. Luke Chapters 22 and 23; and Good Friday, St. John, Chapters 18 and 19. The fact that Penderecki's *St. Luke Passion* received its first performance on the Wednesday of Holy Week (1966) gives evidence that he was well aware of this liturgical practice.

The tradition of setting the Passion story to music seems to have developed as early as the fifth century, when the practice of assigning the Gospels to a different day in Holy Week was first established. The Gospel text of the day was sung by the Priest because singing carried better than speech in the large resonant cathedral. From this time until the fifteenth century the dramatic projection of the story was limited to the simple presentation of the text itself in the appropriate liturgical manner. These Passion texts were chanted by a single singer (*diakon*) who used the different ranges of the voice to present the text that was assigned to the various participants in the Gospel story, thus highlighting the difference between the characters of the story. There is no convincing evidence that the parts were sung by dif-

different people. The words of Christ were sung in the low register, those of the Evangelist, in the middle voice, and the text assigned to the crowd and other characters in the story to the higher range.

By the ninth century, "significant letters" (*litterae significativae*) were used in the manuscript to indicate pitch, tempo and volume. These letters demonstrate that the Passion was approached dramatically at an earlier stage of its development. For example, the words of the Evangelist were set apart by a letter C (*celeriter*), which suggested that the text was to be narrated by the *cronista* or cantor in a flowing style. Those of Christ often bore the letter T (*tenere*) and were to be executed in a slower or held-back manner. The words of the crowd or multitude (*turba*) were most often identified by the letter S (*sursum* or *synagoga*), as well as by A (*altus*), L (*levare*) and F (*fortiter*). These innovations represented an attempt, even in early times, to bring dramatic content to the projection of the story; not only did the various pitch levels contribute to the dramatic intensity of the Passion account, but the several speeds indicated in the old manuscripts helped to establish the personality differences between the characters of the story.

Plainsong Passions

The first report of a Passion performance by more than one person appears in the *Gros livre* (1254) of the Dominicans. Here the words of Christ are recited on the low notes B, A, or c, those of the Evangelist on *f*, and the *turba* passages on high*b* flat. By the fourteenth and fifteenth centuries, the division of the text between three singers and plainsong chanting had become a universal practice. This new
type of Passion form assigned three singers to the task that had in the past been the responsibility of one. The words of Christ were designated for the bass, the narrative sections for the tenor, and the text of the crowd (*turba*) and of the minor characters for high voice (*alto*). In some places the crowd and lesser participants were known by the name *synagoga*. This division of the Passion lesson among three singers became a universal practice during the fourteenth and fifteenth centuries as settings of *plainsong Passions* were composed in England, Germany and Italy.

These various innovations in the practice of performing the Passion text added to the dramatic quality of the form and prepared the way for the polyphonic settings which followed.

Polyphonic Settings of the Passion

The first polyphonic settings of the Passion appear in the fifteenth century as the development of the polyphonic techniques of composition that influence the Masses and motets during this period also leave their mark on the Passion as well. Two main types of polyphonic Passions emerge: *responsorial* and *through-composed*.

In the former type, the narrative sections for the Evangelist, and sometimes Christ, are written in plainsong, while the words of the *turba* (multitude) are set polyphonically, in one of four ways:

1. Polyphony is written only for *turba* sections which are groups of people.

2. Polyphony for all except the Evangelist and the words of Christ.

3. Polyphony for all sections including the words of Christ but excluding the Evangelist.

4. Polyphony for all parts except the Evangelist, including the *exordium* and *conclusio*.

The *through-composed Passion*, on the other hand, is polyphonic throughout, although utterances of individuals might be identified by a thinning of the texture or a similar compositional device. In this type the entire story, including all the different characters, is told by the chorus.

The most significant innovations in the Passion's formal evolution take place within the more dramatic responsorial genre. This is due simply to the fact that the responsorial type is more closely allied to the original liturgical function of the Passion and is therefore more easily incorporated into the worship service. Another reason for its popularity is to be found in its inherent dramatic potential. As with the earliest Passion settings, the "characters" of the drama are easily distinguishable by voice part. As the responsorial form evolved it became increasingly more polyphonic in texture.

While the more dramatic responsorial Passion was the first to be widely used, once the ability to create lengthy sections of polyphony was a common practice of the time, the *through-composed Passion* (or *motet Passion* as it was also commonly known) blossomed forth for a brief period (c. 1560-1630). In this type, in which the complete text including the narration is set polyphonically, three compositional styles may be recognized:

1. Those which set the complete text according to one of the Gospels.

2. Those which take sections from all four Evangelists, including all seven words of Christ on the cross, an *exordium* and a *conclusio*.

3. Those which set a shortened version of the text from one Gospel.

Even in these early Passion settings, it is evident that the account in St. Matthew is used more frequently by composers than any of the other three. The popularity of the St. Matthew version may be attributed to its assigned use on Palm Sunday and to its more dramatic character. It also describes more events of the Passion story and describes them in greater detail. Chart I in Chapter III (p. 00) illustrates the harmony of the Gospels in their description of the Passion account.

The St. Matthew text has one disadvantage, however. It contains only one of the seven words of Christ on the Cross ("My God, my God, why hast Thou forsaken me?"), which are distributed among the other three Gospels; three each in Luke and John and one in Mark. (This topic will be explored in greater depth in Chapter III). Thus, the setting of the text from any one of the Passion accounts provides no opportunity for the composer to include as a group the "Seven Last

Words of the Cross." It was not long, however, until the practice of combining the texts from the four Gospels became a common occurence. One popular text setting that emerged was the "Seven Last Words of the Cross."

This practice of combining the texts from the four Gospels occurs first in a motet-Passion attributed to Antoine de Longueval (fl. 1509-1522), who was active as a composer in France during the first quarter of the sixteenth century. His choice of text is declared in the *Exordium* (the announcement of specific passages to be read) that opens the motet. In this particular work the choir names all four Gospels. The normal practice in the Passion of the time, before and after Longueval, is to introduce the work through this announcement (by the Evangelist in the *responsorial Passion*, and by the choir in a *motet Passion*) of the source of the text in the following manner: *Passio Domini nostri Jesu Christi secundum Matthaeum* (or *Lucam, Marcum, Johannem*, as the case may be). In the German Passions a similar formula preceded the work: *Das Leiden und Sterben unsers Herrn Jesu Christi nach dem heiligen Mattäo* (or *Markus, Lukas, Johann*, etc.)

While the Longueval Passion is the earliest example of a polyphonic work in this genre which combines texts from the four Gospels, the tradition of the harmony of the Gospels can be traced back to earlier times. This practice was popularized in the early fifteenth century (ca. 1420) by the *Monotessaron* of Johannes Gerson. It is interesting to note that in the *St. Luke Passion* Penderecki follows this tradition by combining biblical passages from St. Luke and St. John as well as the Psalms and the Lamentations of Jeremiah. Although the Longueval Passion did not find widespread acceptance in the Catholic countries, since the *summa Passionis* text could not be used as a Gospel lesson within the Mass itself, it was an important model for German composers of the late-sixteenth century. Published by Georg Rhau (1488-1548) in Wittenberg in 1538 under Obrecht's name, the Longueval Passion appeared in over twenty sources in four- and six-part versions.

With the development of choirs in some of the court chapels, composers eventually began to set the *turba* music for chorus. One of the first to do so was Gilles de Binchois (ca. 1400-1460). This form of the Passion, in which plainsong alternated with polyphony, was set by Richard Davy (1467-1516) and William Byrd (1543-1622) in England, by the Italians Giovanni Matteo Arola (no dates available) and Francesco Soriano (1549-1621), by the Spanish Tomás Luis de Victoria (1549-1611) and Francesco Guerrero (1527-1599), by the Frenchmen Claude de Sermisy (c. 1490-1562) and Louis Compère (1455-1518), and by the Netherlander Orlando di Lasso (1532-1594). These works fell within the Roman Catholic tradition and were not intended to make a direct impact on the congregation.

Protestant Passions

Despite these innovations, the most significant developments in the history of the Passion occurred in Germany, especially Protestant Germany, beginning about the third decade of the sixteenth century. The basis for this evolution came from the works of Johann Walter (1496-1570), who composed responsorial settings of the Gospels of all four evangelists as formal models for Protestant church composers. These so-called Walterian Passions, which are regarded not so much as compositions in their own right as examples of how Passions were to be sung within the liturgy, included several notable characteristics:

1. The traditional Passion tones were transformed to fit the German language.

2. The *cantus firmus* was retained as the basis for the choral as well as other sections of the Passion.

3. The *turba* sections, which were composed for chorus, were set in simple four-part polyphony with the Passion tones clearly recognizable.

4. After 1560, the form was expanded to include a polyphonic *exordium* and *conclusio* as well as a Lutheran thanksgiving at the end.

The Passions of Walter, especially his setting of the St. Matthew text, were used as models by Protestant composers well into the eighteenth century. This was the approved form and the only one allowed in the regular Mass service. In his *Deutsche Messe* (1526) Luther spoke out against what he called the *Vierpassion singen*, apparently referring to the *summa Passionis* in which texts from the four Gospels were mixed.

While the *summa Passionis* text was not allowed in Lutheran services, a text of a similar type by Luther's friend, the reformer Johann Bugenhagen, appeared at the same time but was intended to be read, not sung. However, since Bugenhagen's text enjoyed great popularity, as did the responsorial Passion, the monophonic and polyphonic *summa Passionis* in Latin and German soon came into vogue despite Luther's objections.

As the sixteenth century progresses, the model of Walter is modified somewhat. The later composers tend to move away from the strict *cantus firmus* technique and, as became the case in the Italian Passions, a greater number of the sections are set polyphonically. Antonio Scandello (1517-1580) is credited with the first polyphonic setting of the words of Christ in his *St. John Passion* (c. 1560) after the Italian fashion, leaving only the narrative sections of the text monophonic. This work is an example of the mingling of both types within a single composition. And as the polyphonic techniques became further refined, the *motet* or *through-composed Passion*, based on the Longueval Passion, provided a model for this style.

Some through-composed works of the time were set to the shortened version of one of the Gospels (for example, *St. John*), with the inclusion of all "Seven Last Words of the Cross" after the Italian model. These Passions, composed in five rather than three parts, were designed specifically for Protestant worship. It was also characteristic of this type that the *Passion tone* furnished the basis for the polyphonic setting. The *St. John Passion* (1594) of Leonhard Lechner (c. 1553-1606), in which the fifth section gives an exact translation into German of the third section of the *Longueval Passion*, is called by Gustav Reese "perhaps the finest of all the German Passions written in the sixteenth century."[1]

Another example of a typical sixteenth century *motet Passion* is the four-part German Passion of Joachim a Burck (1546-1610). Based on an abridged version of the St. John text, this work includes only the three of the seven last words that appropriately belong to the St. John account. In his musical setting, Burck abandons the passion tones as a basis for his polyphony, thus freeing him to use the techniques of the contemporary motet to their fullest extent. Burck's *St. John Passion* (1568) became the model for most of the later compositions in motet style.

With the *St. John Passion* of Christoph Demantius (1567-1643), the last known setting of the motet Passion form, the effort to establish a distinctive German style reaches its height. Although this work was composed rather well into the seventeenth century (1631), it actually belongs to an earlier style period in which the composer's thorough training in Renaissance polyphony is evident in the skill with which the work is constructed. This six-voice Passion, which is written in three sections, is set entirely in motet style. The regular alternation of brief passages between high and low voices, the astonishing amount of vitality and variety in the writing, and the careful and consistent use of expressive musical ideas brings to the Passion form the type of craftsmanship that is found in later examples by Heinrich Schütz and J. S. Bach.

With the three Passions of Heinrich Schütz (1585-1672) (*St. Matthew*, 1666; *St. Luke*, 1665; and *St. John*, 1666), the responsorial model of Johann Walter serves as a reference point. Although Heinrich Schütz had studied with Giovanni Gabrieli and was significantly influenced by that Venetian master in his earlier works, these austere works indicate a return to a type of Passion common one hundred years earlier. For example, the narrative and dialogue sections return to a kind of plainsong intonation which is interspersed with four voice *turba* choruses. Schütz follows the standard practice of the early German Passion settings by using the traditional recitation tone for the monologues, including the narrative of the Evangelist. Although he had framed powerful choral movements in other works with colorful instrumental resources, in the Passions Schütz dispenses with instruments altogether, including even the continuo. He does not even afford himself the luxury of the modest instrumental recources employed in his earlier *Seven Words of Christ on the Cross* (1645). Written in strict a cappella style, and using only the biblical text of the specific Gospel evangelist, these works employ with extreme economy of means only an unaccompanied solo recitative and the four part *turba* chorus. Yet the variety of treatment is remarkable; behind the simple text settings is a vivid and incisive compositional style that points to similar movements in Bach's Passion.

The oratorio Passion of the seventeenth century

The German Passion tradition was exposed to some exciting innovations in the early seventeenth century with the introduction of the Italian style, and with it the setting of biblical texts to continuous music in oratorio fashion. Developments in Italy, leading to the beginnings of opera and its sacred counterpart, the *oratorio*, began to filter into Germany with the return of students who had begun to compose in this style while working with the Italian masters. The transformation from the dramatic *(responsorial)* and motet *(through-composed)* styles of the late-sixteenth and early-seventeenth centuries to this new Italian style - or at least borrowing freely from elements of that style - was completed with the oratorios of Schütz, but contributions were made by at least two other composers of the period, Ambroius Beber (fl. 1610-1620) and Thomas Selle (1599-1663).

In Beber's *St. Mark Passion* (1610), the characters in the drama are not portrayed by solo voices, as had been the case in the preceding period, but by combinations of voices which were assigned to identifiable characters within the drama. The only voice tone set apart is that of the evangelist, written in plainsong style and composed in expository sections as short as four notes and as long as three hundred. This style adds a necessary abstract clarity to the story, and provides an effective contrast to the choral passages as well. The *Exordium* is set for chorus SATB in note-against-note style, a direct and simple approach to the choral singing that prevails throughout the entire work. For the remainder of the Passion, the *turba* always appears in five parts, SSATB, with the SATB combination generally reserved for the words of Jesus.

The next step in the evolution of the oratorio Passion occurred around 1650 when composers began adding fundamental and ornamental instruments to the delivery of the text. Such settings are broken up by the insertion of reflective episodes, sinfonias, parallel biblical text interpolations, and hymn tunes. The earliest works to fall into this category were those of Thomas Selle (1599-1663). His *St. Matthew Passion* (1642) includes scoring for the continuo throughout the work and deploys a large group of instruments to give individuality to the characters and to create Venetian effects in the *turba* choruses. Whereas Beber had identified each character in the drama by associating it with a combination of voices, Selle characterized each of his soloists by adding a unique accompanying group; the Evangelist by two bassoons, Jesus by two violins and bassoon, the Maid by three violins without continuo, Peter and the Servant by two recorders and bassoon, and Pilate by two cornetti and one trombone.

As a general rule, in the first half of the seventeenth century instruments were still used rather sparingly in Passion settings. The primary focus of the Passion continued to be liturgical, specifically the liturgy of Holy Week, and the use of instruments at this time of the church year was considered inappropriate. This may be considered the primary reason why Schütz's music for this season of the year is a model of restraint. Only one of his compositions for Holy Week, *The Seven Last Words of Christ on the Cross* (1645), makes use of instruments. The instrumentation is unspecified, but it is thought that Schütz intended string instruments. The practice of omitting exact designations for instruments stems from the past, and appears to be a deliberate return to the style that existed before the Venetian influence made itself felt in works of this genre.

An important step in the evolution of the form was to incorporate the Italian *sinfonia* into the Passion structure. It was about 1665 in the North German regions of Braunschweig und Lüneburg that settings appear with instrumental accompaniments to both the arias and sinfonias. This oratorio-like expansion of the form, first occurring in the Wolfenbüttel *St. Matthew Passion* of Martin Colerus, consisted of biblical passages in connection with the Last Supper, sinfonias (some with chorale tunes), old chorales as the basis for arias, Latin text insertions, and the incorporation of contemporay hymn tunes.

The transition between the responsorial and Oratorio Passion can be seen clearly in the *St. Matthew Passion* of the Lüneburg composer, Christian Flor. In this work we find many of the characteristics that appear in the eighteenth century. The Evangelist and other individuals are set in *plainsong* passages which are *rhetorical in nature*. The *turba* choruses are accompanied by flutes, viols, and continuo. There are also interpolations of instrumental passages and vocal arias at key points in the first half to balance the crowd interruptions in the second half of these two part works.

The final step in the evolution of the oratorio Passion occurs at the end of the seventeenth century. In a *St. Matthew Passion* by Johann Sebastiani (1622-1683), there is a more diversified use of instruments, especially in the solo sections. Among the interesting features in this work are the assignment of specific instrumental accompaniments to the leading characters and the inclusion of chorale stanzas for solo voice with accompaniment. While on some occasions the Evangelist sings with continuo only, the part is usually accompanied by two *viole da gamba* (or *da braccio*) and *viola bassa*. A third viola is added for the chorales and SATB choruses. The words of Jesus are set to two violins and continuo; the same treatment of the text as used by J. S. Bach in 1723 in his *St. John Passion*. The *turba* sections are supported by the full instrumental group. While this work cannot be classified as a true eighteenth century oratorio *Passion* because it lacks arias and choruses that expand upon the biblical story, the inclusion of chorale verses brings it one step closer to the famous form of the Bach Passions.

Hamburg, which had seen the first German imitation of Venetian musical splendor, witnessed early attempts at sacred opera and operatic settings of the Passion, based on new libretti that paraphrased rather than borrowed phrases from the Bible. These experiments paved the way for the development of the Passion oratorio in the eighteenth century.

The Passion in the eighteenth century

Classification of the eighteenth century Passion is made extremely difficult by the many different forms which were written; however, four basic types can be identified:

1. The traditional seventeenth century *responsorial Passion* without instruments was still written, but was more or less ignored by the best composers. This was primarily the liturgical form of the Passion.

2. The more artistic *oratorio Passion*, which still adhered to the biblical text but included poetic textual interpolations, flourished under J.S. Bach and Georg Philipp Telemann.

3. The *Passion oratorio* with completely original text gained immediate popularity with North German composers because of its operatic style.

4. The lyrical *Passion meditation* in oratorio form without direct dialogue from the biblical Evangelists was popular in the second half of the century. These works can be considered essentially Easter histories.

By far the most important types to emerge in the eighteenth century were the *Passion oratorio* and the *oratorio Passion*, the latter also known as "Passions-Music" coupled with the name of the Gospel from which it was derived.

The first work to become known as a *Passion oratorio* was Reinhard Keiser's *Der blutige und sterbende Jesus* (1704). Here for the first time in the history of the Passion the text is the work of a poet. The Evangelist is omitted and the traditional Gospel narrative of the Passion story is replaced by a paraphrase which departs significantly from the Biblical account. The poet, Christian Friedrich Hunold (1681-1721), established a trend which proved to be popular with the opera-obsessed composers and audiences in Hamburg in the early eighteenth century. In spite of unfavorable reactions by the liturgical authorities to the theatrical elements in these works, many other composers took up this pattern. At this point in its development, the Passion and the opera came as close to uniting as they ever would. The following excerpt from *Grove's Dictionary* (1955 edition) describes one such work:

> In 1704 the Passion succumbed to the popular inclination to dramatize Biblical stories, in a setting by Reinhard Keiser (1674-1739) of Christian Friedrich Hunold-Menantes's "Der blutige und sterbende Jesus," an "Oratorio musicalish gesetz." The libretto, rhymed throughout, contained no chorales and dispensed with the biblical narrative. The author cast the work in the form of three "cantatas" or "Soliloquia": the Lamentations of Mary Magdalene; the Tears of Peter; the Love-song of Zion's Daughter, a character later adopted by Brockes, Picander and Bach. Its theatrical music and the elimination of the Biblical narrative invited grave displeasure, and even public condemnation by one of the Hamburg clergy.[2] (585)

To conservative minds, these *Passion oratorios* contained "the spirit of opera more than God's word," with the effect of "ear tickling" rather than "edification," and they were little used in divine worship. These Passions established a new trend in choral performance: they were works on sacred topics which eventually found their way into the concert hall rather than the house of worship.

J.S. Bach (1685-1750) probably wrote five Passions, if the accounts of his second son, Carl Philipp Emanuel and the organist-composer L. J. F. Agricola, his student for three years, are accurate, but only two of these survive: *St. John* (1723) and *St. Matthew* (1729). These works represent some of his best compositional efforts. The two Passions are different in their degrees of musical complexity and in the manner in which their texts approach the drama of the Crucifixion.

Like his *Christmas Oratorio*, Bach's Passions fall somewhere between the oratorio Passion, the Responsorial Passion History, and the Passion Oratorio. Practical considerations placed this type of Passion between music for the church service and music for the concert hall. In these works the narrative of Christ's suffering remained the central feature despite the influence of the Italian and North German Passions of the seventeenth century. Bach was willing to accept elements from opera in his cantatas and cantata-like oratorios, but they were always subordinate to the needs of the whole work.

The texts of Bach's Passions fall into three categories: the Biblical narrative taken from Luther's translation of the New Testament, Lutheran chorales from the *Geistliches Gesangbüchlein* (1524), and interpolated free-text choruses, arias, ariosos and recitatives by the poets Barthold Heinrich Brockes and Christian

Heinrich Postel in the *St. John Passion* and Christian Friedrich Henrici (1700-1764), better known by the pseudonym Picander, who provided all the poems for the *St. Matthew Passion*.

The earlier *St. John Passion* (1722-1723) is relatively simple in its musical material. The narration of the Evangelist, as well as the parts of the characters, is supported only by the continuo; the *turba* sections are entirely resticted to four-part chorus; the numerous chorales vitalized the story for the congregation who were not expected to participate in the singing, but were to apply the drama to their own theological milieu. Not only does the participation of the congregation lack any precedent in the music before Bach's time, but the deviations from the simplest settings of the chorale tunes and the frequent appearance of four-part settings indicate that the attention was centered on the choir and not the congregation.

The *St. Matthew Passion* (1729) is complex in its performing forces - two orchestras and two choruses in addition to the soloists - but it is simple and unaffected in its expression. The usual division into two parts, that sung before the sermon being considerably shorter than that following it, is present as it was in the *St. John Passion*. The use of the trio sonata accompaniment to the words of Jesus, though distinctive, was not a new concept with Bach, as noted earlier in the discussion of the *St. Matthew Passion* of Sebastiani.

The lyrical passages and symbolic roles found in the German Passion oratorio were models for the fourth type of Passion found in the eighteenth century, the lyrical *Passion meditation* in oratorio form. It is represented in Italy and italianized Germany from 1730 on by Metastasio's *La Passione di Gesu Christi* set by Caldara, Jommelli, Paisiello and others. An increasing aversion to operatic qualities in sacred music, aesthetic objections to sung narratives and dialogues, and the general excess of feeling in the age of sentiment favored the development of this type in Evangelical parts of Germany. As early as 1720 it is discernible in several Passions by G. H. Stölzel, Kapellmeister of Gotha, but is best exemplified by *Tod Jesu* (1755) by Carl Heinrich Graun (1704-1759). After its first performance in Berlin on March 26, 1755, *Tod Jesu* enjoyed considerable success for two reasons: it presented the Passion story as it reflected the image of a sensitive and contemplative Christ; and it used the simplified musical language of pre-Classicism. No other setting of K. W. Ramler's libretto was able to compete with Grauns's, not even Telemann's (1755). Its influence seems to have marked an important departure in the history of the Passion similar to those initiated earlier by the works of Longueval, Walter, Burck and Scandello.

Nineteenth and twentieth century Passions

With the advent of public concerts, choral societies and music festivals in the nineteenth century, the Passion was considered more a concert piece than a liturgical work. Beethoven's *Christ on the Mount of Olives* (1803), known primarily as a concert work, was performed in many Protestant areas of Germany. The Penderecki *St. Luke Passion* falls within this tradition of music for concert rather than liturgical performance.

Even in the middle of the nineteenth century, the Passion music of J. S. Bach was influential in the manner in which this text was set. The growing familiarity with the monumental *St. Matthew Passion*, as the result of Felix Mendelssohn's famous performance in 1829, had the astounding effect of inhibiting the writing of new Passion settings and eventually influenced the writing of new works, either directly or indirectly. In time the *St. Matthew Passion* became the absolute standard, even though performed primarily on the concert stage. Ironically, the church could offer no adequate competitor and only a few new compositions in the oratorio Passion genre entered the repertory.

This situation began to change only after the revival of interest in the older music of the Renaissance (Cecilian movement in the Catholic Church) and Baroque (the models of Heinrich Schütz) became evident. One example of the influence of the older forms is found in *Die Passion* (1896) by the Austrian Heinrich von Herzogenberg (1843-1900). Although a Catholic, he devoted himself to the composition of music for Protestant worship during the last years of his life as a result of the encouragement of Johannes Brahms (1833-1897). Based on a text compiled by the theologian Friedrich Spitta, this work consists of a series of biblical recitatives (based on Protestant chorales), set in a manner frequently reminiscent of Schütz, together with polyphonic chorales in sixteenth century style, biblical motets in the spirit of the seventeenth century, aria-like choruses in the eighteenth century manner, together with the inclusion of congregational chorales. This was music for the congregation, written in reaction to the Passion oratorios which were designed for concert audiences.

The first composer of the twentieth century to return to an earlier model was the Leipzig *Thomaskirche* cantor Kurt Thomas (1904-1973). Pointing backward to Leonhard Lechner's *St. John Passion* (1594),[3] Thomas' *Passionsmusik nach dem Evangelisten Markus* (1926) was composed for mixed chorus a cappella. Based exclusively on chapters 14 and 15 of the gospel of St. Mark, this work dispenses with reflective interludes, soloists and instruments, and presents the drama of the Passion solely through the medium of a vivid polyphonic vocal setting.

The most thoroughly devoted of all the twentieth century composers to the ideals of Heinrich Schütz was the German Hugo Distler (1908-1942). Upon hearing a Good Friday performance of Schütz's *St. Matthew Passion* in Lübeck, Distler was moved to compose a "representation of the Passion story . . . in raiment appropriate to the time . . . but in the spirit of the early a cappella Passion as it culminated in Schütz."[4] This work, entitled *Choral Passion* (1933) and based on the composer's own selection from the four Gospels, is a choral variation on *Jesu deine Passion*. The hymn verses of the chorale variations, which open the composition and close each of its sections, are derived from various Passion melodies. The chorale tune *Christus, der uns selig macht*, serves as the cantus firmus for all eight reflective chorale motets, thus unifying the work both internally and externally. The recitatives, always in the manner of speech, make use of the traditional registers; the Evangelist is a tenor, Christ is a bass, the high priest a high tenor, and the voices of Judas, Pilate, and the thief are represented by a bass in the chorus. Friedrich Blume speaks to the importance of this work when he writes: "The artistic significance of this responsorial Passion rests in its primarily five-part chorale motets and in the terse and powerful effect of the people's choruses, which seek to emulate Schütz and are as resolute as they are bold in their search for hard, dramatic realism through the use of clashing seconds and passages in fourths and fifths."[5]

The *St. Matthew Passion* (1949-1950) of Ernst Pepping (1901-1980) also occupies a significant place in the history of the twentieth century Passion. This work follows in the tradition of the polyphonic motet Passion of Kurt Thomas. Utilizing the resources of double chorus, it portrays the account of Christ's sufferings from the betrayal by Judas to the Crucifixion. The two choruses assume different roles: chorus I delivers the report of the events; chorus II offers reflection, depth, meaning, and participation, joining with chorus I in the double choruses of the Introduction, *Intermedium*, and Finale motets, and at key points in the Passion narrative where the two choruses are combined to intensify the drama. It is based on free tonality, occasionally expanded to polytonality, and is unified by its devotion to the truth and reality of the Gospel narrative.

Most of the recent Passion settings are of the responsorial Passion type established by Walter, developed by Schütz and first revived by Distler. Many are unaccompanied. They include unaccompanied monodic recitatives and polyphonic *turba* choruses, and, as a rule, chorale settings constitute the opening and closing movements. The majority of these twentieth century Passion compositions are written by Protestant composers in Germany, all of which makes Penderecki's Latin setting of the St. Luke Passion all the more unusual and original.

Notes

[1] Gustav Reese, *Music in the Renaissance*, revised edition (New York: W. W. Norton and Co., 1959), 688.

[2] *Grove's Dictionary of Music and Musicians*, 5th ed., s.v. "Passion Music; (4) The Oratorio Passion." by Charles Sanford Terry.

[3] When this work was first performed in Germany, it created a sensation and made the twenty-two year old composer a celebrity almost overnight. After its initial success, however, this Passion failed to live up to its promise. It is virtually forgotten today. This does not minimize its historical significance, however, as a work which pointed the listener to the earlier model, the *St. John Passion* (1594) of Leonhard Lechner.

[4] Friedrich Blume, *Protestant Church Music*, translation copy (New York: W. W. Norton and Co., 1974), 454.

[5] Ibid., p. 455.

Chapter III

THE TEXT OF THE ST. LUKE PASSION

Penderecki's reasons for selecting the St. Luke text over the accounts in the other Gospels were explained at a press conference which took place in the City Hall of Münster on the day of the world premiere, March 30, 1966.[1] When asked why he had chosen the Third Gospel, he answered: "Not only for literary reasons, on account of the especially beautiful language, but rather because there had indeed already been two unusually good Passion compositions based on Matthew and John."[2] It is the purpose of this chapter to study the text of the *Passion* in detail. We will begin with an overview of the St. Luke account.

An Overview of the St. Luke Account

In its dramatic structure and its broad presentation of the various events surrounding the death of Christ, the account in St. Luke actually differs very little from the events which appear in Matthew and Mark. Each of the first three Gospels begins the Passion story with the plotting of the chief priests (Matthew 26:3-5; Mark 14:1-2; and Luke 22:2), while the shorter account in St. John commences the Passion narrative with the betrayal and arrest of Jesus (John 18:2-9) and omits entirely the important preliminary scenes of the Last Supper and the Agony in the Garden of Gethsemane (for a comparison of the four Passion texts, see Chart I, "The Passion Account in the Four Gospels").

Of the four Gospels, the story in St. Matthew is perhaps the richest in pictorial detail, including as it does the accounts of Judas' remorse and death, the dream of Jesus which troubles Pilate's wife, and the governor's symbolic washing of his hands. It is thus not difficult to understand why composers throughout the ages have chosen the St. Matthew text more than any other for musical settings of the Passion story. St. Luke's Gospel, which has generally been neglected by composers, includes two scenes which are not dealt with in any detail in the other Gospels: the Way of the Cross and the scene of Jesus between the two thieves.

The Text Chosen by Penderecki

When considered from the standpoint of its biblical sources, the Latin text chosen by the composer consists of ten passages from St. Luke's Gospel (Chapters 22 and 23), three from St. John (Chapter 19) and Old Testament excerpts from Psalms 10, 15, 22, 31, and 56 and the Lamentations of Jeremiah. Nonbiblical text interpolations include the hymn "Vexilla regis prodeunt," the *Improperia*, the hymn "Pangua lingua" (Antiphons 1 und 2) and the sequence "Stabat Mater" (verses 1, 3, 5, 10), taken directly from the Roman liturgy. It should also be noted here that it is the composer's intention that the work be performed in Latin. A statement to this effect appears on the title page of the *Passion*.

39

Chart I

THE ACCOUNT OF THE FOUR GOSPELS
(The harmony of the Gospels)

St. Matthew (Ch. 26-27)	*St. Mark (Ch. 14-15)*
1. Jesus announces his own impending crucifixion two days before Passover (26:1-2)	
2. Chief priests seek to destroy Jesus (26:3,4,5)	1. Chief priests seek to destroy Jesus (14:1)
3. Jesus is anointed with precious ointment (26:6-12)	2. Jesus is anointed with precious ointment (14:3-9)
4. Judas plans to betray Jesus (26:14-16)	3. Judas plans to betray Jesus (14:10'11)
5. The disciples prepare the Passover (26:17-19)	4. The disciples prepare the Passover (14:12-16)
6. The Last Supper (26:20-29)	5. The Last Supper (14:17-25)
7. The ascent to the Mount of Olives	6. The ascent to the Mount of Olives (14:26-31)
8. The agony in the Garden (26:36-46)	7. The agony in the Garden (14:32-42)
9. The arrest of Jesus (26:47-56)	8. The arrest of Jesus (14:43-50)
10. The hearing before Caiaphas (26:57-75)	9. The hearing before the chief priest (14:53-65)
11. Peter's denial and remorse (26:69-75)	10. Peter's denial and remorse (14:66-72)
12. Judas' repentance and death (27:3-10)	
13. The trial before Pilate (27:11-14)	11. The trial before Pilate (15:1-5)
14. The soldiers crown Jesus with thorns (27:27-32)	12. The soldiers crown Jesus with thorns (15:16-23)
15. The Crucifixion (27:33-44)	13. The Crucifixion (16:22-23)
16. The death of Jesus (27:45-50)	14. The death of Jesus (16:33-37)
17. The descent from the Cross and burial (27:57-61)	15. The burial (15:42-47)
18. The chief priests demand the sealing of the tomb	

St. Luke (Ch. 22-23)	St. John (Ch. 18-19)
1. Chief priests seek to destroy Jesus (22:2)	
2. Judas plans to betray Jesus (22:3-6)	
3. The disciples prepare the Passover (22:7-13)	
4. The Last Supper (22:14-30)	
5. The Ascent to the Mount of Olives (22:39)	
6. The agony in the Garden (22:40-46)	
7. The arrest of Jesus (22:47-53)	1. The arrest of Jesus (18:2-11)
8. The hearing before the chief priest (22:54) 22:66-71)	2. The hearing before the chief priest (18:12, 19-24)
9. Peter's denial and remorse (22:54-62)	3. Peter's denial (18:15-18; 25-27)
10. The trial before Pilate and Herod (23:1-25)	4. The trial before Pilate (18:25-27, 33-38, 19:11-15)
11. The way of the cross (23:26-32)	5. The soldiers crown Jesus with thorns (19:2-3)
12. The Crucifixion (23:33-43)	6. The Crucifixion (19:11-24)
	7. There stood beneath the Cross (19:25'27)
13. The death of Jesus (23:44-46)	8.The death of Jesus (19:28-30)
14. The burial (23:50-56)	9. The descent from the Cross and the burial (19:31-42)

Following the tradition of the German Passions of the seventeenth century, which were based on the dramatic structure of the early Italian oratorios, and similar in contruction to the Bach Passions, the Penderecki *St. Luke Passion* is divided into two nearly equal parts. In the liturgical tradition, in which the interval between the two halves is occupied by a sermon on the subject of the Passion, the break in St. Matthew's account is usually made after the scene of Peter's denial of Christ, a logical division because it comes after the twenty-sixth chapter. The equivalent interval in St. John's gospel comes at the end of the eighteenth chapter, where Pilate gives the crowd the opportunity to choose between Jesus and Barabbas. Penderecki divides Parts I and II at the same place, and the first half ends with the ringing cry of the crowd, "Crucify him, Crucify him."

The gospel text in the Latin of the Vulgate, which establishes the basic structure for the drama of the Passion, is mostly narrated by the Speaker in the role of the Evangelist with some assistance from the chorus. The baritone soloist sings the words of Christ, while the remaining participants in the drama - Peter, Pilate, and, above all, the crowd - are taken by the bass soloist and the choir.

The Gospel Narrative Taken from Luke and John

Penderecki picks up the account of St. Luke with Jesus praying on the Mount of Olives (Scene 1), Luke 22:39-44: [movement 2]

Et egressus ibat secundum consuetudinem in montem Olivarum	*And he came out, and went, as he was wont, to the Mount of Olives,*
Secuti sunt autem illum et discipuli. . . positis genibus orabat dicens: Pater, si vis, transfer calicem istum a me: verumtamen non mea voluntas, sed Tua fiat. Apparuit autem illi angelus de caelo, confortans eum. Et factus in agonia prolixius orabat. Et factus est sudor eius sicut guttae sanguinis decurrentis in terram.	*And his disciples also followed him - And he kneeled down, and prayed, saying: Father if thou be willing, remove this cup from me: nevertheless not my will, but thine be done." And there appeared an angel unto him from heaven, strengthening him. And being in an agony he prayed more earnestly: and his sweat was as it were great drops of blood falling down to the ground.*

St. Luke 22:39-44

The arrest of Jesus follows (Scene 2), Luke 22:47-53: [movement 5]

Adhuc eo loquente ecco turba, et qui vocabatur Iudas, unus de duodecim, antecedebat eos et appropinquavit Iesu ut oscularetur eum . . .	*And while he yet spake, behold a multitude, and he that was called Judas, one of the twelve, went before them, and*

Iuda, osculo Filium hominis tradis? . . . Quasi ad latronem existis cum gladiis et fustibus? . . . sed haec est hora vestra et potestas tenebrarum.	kissed him. But Jesus said unto him: "Judas, betrayest thou the Son of Man with a kiss? . . . Be ye come out, as against a thief, with swords and staves? But this is your hour, and the power of darkness."

Luke 22:47-53

Peter's denial of Christ forms the basis for the next scene (Scene 3), Luke 22:54-62: [movement 8]

Comprehendentes autem eum duxerunt ad domum principis sacerdotum. Petrus vero sequebatur a longe . . . Quem cum vidasset ancilla quaedam sedentem ad lumen et eum fuisset intuita, dixit: Et hic cum illo erat . . . Mulier, non novi illum. Et post pusillum alius videns eum dixit: Et tu de illis es . . . O homo, non sum. Et intervallo facto quasi horae unius, alius quidam affirmabat dicens: Vere et hic cum illo erat; nam et Galilaeus est. . . . Homo, nesevo, quid dicis. Et continuo adhuc illo loquente cantavit gallus. Et conversus Dominus respexit Petrum. Et recordatus est Petrus verbi Domini . . . Et egressus foras . . . flevit amare.	Then they took him, and led him, and brought him into the high priest's house. And Peter followed afar off. But a certain maid beheld him as he sat by the fire, and earnestly looked upon him, and said: "This man also was with him." "Woman, I know him not." And after a little while another saw him, and said: "Thou are also of them." "Man, I am not." And about the space of one hour another confidently affirmed, saying: "Of a truth, this fellow also was with him: for he is a Galilaean." "Man, I know not what thou sayest." And immediately, while he yet spake, the cock crew. And the Lord turned, and looked upon Peter. And Peter remembered the word of the Lord. And he went out and wept bitterly.

Luke 22:54-62

The text from Luke 22:63-70 provides the setting of the next scene (Scene 4): the mocking before the High Priest. [movement 10]

Et viri, qui tenebant illum, illudebant ei caedentes. Et velaverunt eum et per- cutiebant faciem eius et interrogebant	And the men that held Jesus mocked him, and smote him. And when they had blindfolded him, they struck him on the face,

43

eum dicentes: *Prophetiza, quis est qui te percussit? . . . Tu ergo es Filius Dei? Vos dicitis, quia ego sum.*

and asked him: saying: "Prophesy, who is it that smote thee?" "Art thou then the Son of God?" "Ye say that I am."

Luke 22:63-70

The account of Jesus before Pilate and Herod in Luke 23:1-22 concludes Part I of the Passion (Scene 5): [movement 13]

Et surgens omnis multitudo corum duxerunt illum ad Pilatum. Coeperunt autem illum accusare dicentes: Hunc invenimus subvertentem gentem nostram et prohi-

bentem tributa dare Caesari et dicentem se Christum regem esse. . . . Tu es rex Iudaeorum? Tu dices. Nihil invenio causae in hoc homine . . . Et . . . remisit eum ad Herodem . . . Herodes autem . . . interrogabat, . . . eum multis sermonibus. At ipse nihil illi respondebat . . . Sprevit autem illum Herodes . . . et . . . indutum veste alba . . . remisit ad Pilatum . . . Pilatus autem convocatis principibus sacerdotum . . ., dixit ad illos:

. . . ecce nihil dignum morte actum est ei. Emendatum ergo illum dimittam. Tolle hunc et dimitte nobis Barabbam . . . Iterum autem Pilatus locutus est ad eos volens dimittere Iesum. At illi succlamabant dicentes: Crucifige, crucifige illum . . . Quid enim mali fecit iste? Nullam causam mortis invenio in eo.

And the whole multitude of them arose, and led him unto Pilate. And they began to accuse him, saying: "We found this fellow perverting the nation, and forbidding to give tribute to Caesar, saying that he himself is Christ a King." "Art thou the King of the Jews?" "Thou sayest it." "I find no fault in this man." And he sent him to Herod. Herod questioned with him in many words; but he answered him nothing. And Herod set him at nought, and mocked him, and arrayed him in a gorgeous robe, and sent him again to Pilate. And Pilate when he had called together the chief priests, said unto them: "Nothing worthy of death is done unto him. I will therefore chastise him, and release him." "Away with this man, and release unto us Barabbas." Pilate, therefore, willing to release Jesus, spake again to them. But they cried, saying: "Crucify him, crucify him." Why, what evil hath he done?" I have found no cause of death in him."

St. Luke 23:1-22

The scene of the Crucifixion is divided between the passages in John and Luke. However, Penderecki chooses the more vivid description in St. John to identify the location (Scene 6): [movement 15]

Et baiulans sibi crucem exivit in eum, qui dicitur Calvariae, locum, Hebraice autem Golgotha.

And he bearing his cross went forth into a place called the place of the skull, which is called in the Hebrew "Golgotha."

St. John 19:17

After the *Improperia*, he concludes the scene with the account in the Third Gospel, Luke 23:33, but uses only the second half of the verse: [movement 17]

Ibi crucifixerunt eum et latrones, unum a dextris et alterum a sinistris.	*There they crucified him, and the malefactors, one on the right hand, and the other on the left.*
	St. Luke 23:33

The first of the Seven Words from the Cross ("Father, forgive them, for they know not what they do.") continues the Gospel narrative, Luke 23:34 (Scene 8) [movement 19]

Iesus autem dicebat, Pater, dimitte illis; non enim sciunt, quid faciunt: Dividentes vero vestimenta eius miserunt sortes.	*Then said Jesus: "Father, forgive them, for they know not what they do." And parted they his raiment, and cast lots.*
	St. Luke 23:34

The text for the dramatic mocking of Christ on the Cross (Scene 9) is taken from Luke 23:35-37: [movement 21]

Et stabat populus spectans, et deridebant eum principes cum eis dicentes: Alios salvos fecti, se salvum faciat,	*And the people stood beholding. And the rulers also with them deriding him saying: "He saved others; let him save himself,*
si hic est Christus electus. Illudebant autem ei et milites accendentes et acetum offerentes ei et dicentes: Si tu es rex Iudaeorum, salvum te fac.	*if he be Christ, the chosen of God." And the soldiers also mocked him, coming to him, and offering him vinegar, and saying: "If thou be the king of the Jews save thyself."*
	St. Luke 23:35-37

The narrative of Jesus between the two Thieves (Scene 10) is followed by the second of the Seven Words from the Cross ("Verily I say unto thee, today thou shalt be with me in Paradise"), Luke 23:39-43: [movement 22]

Unus autem de his qui pendebant latronibus blasphemabat eum dicens: Si tu es Christus salvum fac temetipsum et nos. Respondens autem alter increpabat eum dicens: Neque tu times Deum, quod in eadem damnations es. Et nos	*And one of the malefactors which were hanged railed on him, saying: "If thou be Christ, save thyself and us." But the other answering rebuked him saying: "Dost not thou fear God, seeing thou art in the condemnation? And we indeed justly; for we*
quidem iuste, nam digna factis recipimus; hic vero nihil mali gessit . . . Domine, memento mei, cum veneris in regnum	*receive the due rewards of our deeds: but this man hath done*

45

Tuum.   Amen dico tibi: Hodie
mecum eris in paradiso.

nothing amiss. Lord, remember me
when thou comest into thy king-
dom." "Verily I say unto thee,
today thou shalt be with me in
paradise."

St. Luke 23:39-43

Because the scene at the foot of the Cross (Scene 11) appears only in the John
account, Penderecki interpolates the passage from John 19:25-27 at this point in
the narrative. The third of the Seven Words of the Cross ("Woman, behold thy
son!") is heard at the conclusion of this scene. [movement 23]

Stabant autem iuxta crucem Iesu mater
eius et soror matris eius Maria Cleophae
et Maria Magdalene. Cum vidisset ergo
Iesus matrem et discipulum stantem,
quem diligebat, dicit matri suae: Mulier,
ecce filius tuus. Deinde dicit discipulo:
Ecce mater tua.

Now there stood by the cross of
Jesus his mother and his mother's
sister, Mary the wife of Cleophas,
and Mary Magdalene. When Jesus
therefore saw his mother, and the
disciple standing by, whom he
loved, he said unto his mother:
"Woman, behold thy son." Then
saith he to the disciple: "Behold
thy mother!"

St. John 19:25-27

Like the earlier passage in which the description of the Crucifixion is divided
between the accounts of Luke and John, the scene of the Death of Christ is also
presented in a similar manner. The description of the scene (Scene 12) and the
quote from the sixth of the Seven Words of the Cross ("Father, into thy hands I
commend my spirit") are taken from Luke 23:44-46: [movement 25, beginning]

Erat autem fere hora sexta, et tenebrae
factae sunt in universam terram usque
in horam nonam. Et obscuratus est sol,
et velum templi scissum est medium.
Et clamans voce magna Iesus ait: Pater,
in manus Tuas commendo spiritum

meum. Et haec dicens exspiravit.

And it was the sixth hour, and
there was a darkness over all the
earth until the ninth hour. And
the sun was darkened, and the veil
of the temple was rent in the
midst. And when Jesus had cried
with a loud voice, he said: "Father, into thy hands I commend
my spirit." And having said thus,
he gave up the ghost.

St. Luke 23:44-46

The seventh of the Last Words of the Cross ("It is finished.") is quoted from
John 19:30: [movement 25, conclusion]

Consummatum est.

"It is finished."

St. John 19:30

In the tradition of the Longueval Passion[3], Penderecki incorporates passages from six of the Seven Last Words of the Cross in his Passion text. Since these Words of the Cross are distributed throughout the four Gospels, and no single account includes more than three, it is necessary for Penderecki to take them from biblical writings other than St. Luke. Here the composer makes an interesting textual interpolation: for two of his Words of the Cross (Words No. 4 and No. 7), he selects parallel passages in the Old Testament ("My God, my God, why hast thou forsaken me," Psalm 22:1; and for the final appearance of the seventh word, "Into thine hand I commit my spirit," Psalm 31:5).[4] He takes the others from St. Luke and St. John: "Father, forgive them for they know not what they do" Word No. 1 (Luke 23:34); "Today thou shalt be with me in paradise" Word No. 2 (Luke 23:43); "Woman, behold thy son!" Word No. 3 (John 19:26); "Father, into thy hands I commend my spirit" Word No. 6 (Luke 23:46) and "It is finished" Word No. 7 (John 19:30). The only one that does not appear in the Penderecki text is the fifth word, "I thirst" (John 19:28).

As a guide to the study of the St. Luke Passion text, Chart II below identifies the Seven Last Words of the Cross as they appear in the four Gospel accounts.

Chart II

BIBLICAL DERIVATION OF THE SEVEN LAST WORDS ON THE CROSS

Word	Matthew	Mark	Luke	John
1. "Father, forgive them"			23:34	
2. "Today thou shalt be with me in Paradise"			23:43	
3. "Woman, behold thy son"				19:26
4. "My God, my God, why hast thou forsaken me?"	27:46	15:34		
5. "I thirst"				19:28
6. "Father, into thy hands I commend my spirit"			23:46	
7. "It is finished"				19:30

Old Testament Inclusions

The composer's use of excerpts from the *Psalms* and the *Lamentations of Jeremiah* give indication of his keen grasp of biblical literature as well as his ability to tie together the New Testament Passion story with the vivid picture of death by crucifixion that is painted in Psalm 22. The cry of Jesus, "My God, my God, why hast thou forsaken me," the fourth of the Seven Words from the Cross, does not appear in the Luke account. It is included in Matthew and Mark but not in the other two gospels. The description of the Crucifixion as it appears in Psalm 22, written approximately 1,000 years before Christ, is remarkable in that it is so specific concerning the details of this form of execution, expecially so when it is recognized that crucifixion was a Roman, not a Jewish, practice. Penderecki interpolates this Old Testament passage in Scene 1, while Jesus is praying in the Garden. [movement 2]

Deus, Deus mus, respice in me,	*My God, My God, (look upon me)*
quare me dereliquisti?	*Why hast thou forsaken me?*
Deus meus, clamabo per diem,	*O my God, I cry in the daytime,*
et non exaudies.	*but thou hearest not.*
Verba mea auribus percipe, Domine;	*Give ear to my words, O Lord,*
intellige clamorem meum.	*consider my meditation.*

Psalm 22:1-2; 5:1

Psalm 15 serves as the text for the "Domine" aria which concludes Scene 1. [movement 4]

Domine, quis habitabit in taber-	*Lord, who shall abide in thy*
nacula tuo,	*tabernacle?*
Aut quis requiscet in monte sancto tuo?	*Who shall dwell in thy holy hill?*
In pace . . . dormiam . . .	*I will both lay me down and sleep.*
. . . et caro mea requiescet in spe.	*My flesh also shall rest in hope.*

Psalm 15:1; 4:8; 16:9

The short phrase, "Why standest thou afar off, O Lord?", taken from the first verse of Psalm 10, forms the textual basis for the short a cappella movement that concludes Scene 2. [movement 7]

Ut quid, Domine, recessisti longe?	*Why standest thou afar off,*
	O Lord?

Psalm 10:1

It is interesting to note that Penderecki, who put together the various text sources for the *St. Luke Passion*, has included the first verse of Psalm 43, a passage he had also chosen for the third movement of his first published choral work, the *Psalms of David* (1958). The aria on the text, "Indica me, Deus, et discerne causam meam." concludes Scene 3. [movement 4].

Indica me, Deus, et discerne	*Judge me, O God, and plead*
causam meam.	*my cause.*

Psalm 43:1

The touching a cappella Psalm movement which closes Scene 4, is taken from Psalm 56. It refers to a time when the Psalmist fled to the Philistines in fear of Saul and shows the importance of his reliance on God. [movement 12]

Miserere mei, Deus, quoniam concul- cavit me homo, tota die impugnans tribulavit me.	Be merciful to me, O God, for man would swallow me up; he fighting daily oppresseth me.
	Psalm 56:2

Excerpts from Psalm 22 appear twice in Part II of the Passion. In the opening movement, Penderecki quotes from Psalm 22:15: [movement 14)

Et in pulverem mortis deduxisti me.	Thou hast brought me into the dust of death.
	Psalm 22:15

The next four verses of Psalm 22 then form the basis for the lovely a cappella movement that completes Scene 8. [movement 20]

In pulverem mortis deduxisti me	Thou hast brought me into the dust of death.
fonderunt manus meas et pedes meos	They pierced my hands and my feet.
Dinumeraverunt omnia ossa mea, ipsi vero consideraverunt et inspexerunt me.	I may tell all my bones: they look and stare upon me.
Diviserunt sibi vestimenta mea et super vestem meam miserunt sor- tem.	They part my garments among them and cast lots upon my vesture.
Te autem, Domine, ne elongaveris auxilium	But be not thou far from me, O Lord.
Tuum a me;	O my strength, haste thee to help
Ad defensionem meam conspice.	me.
	Psalm 22:15-19

Penderecki closes the Passion with a Psalm of hope based on verses 1, 2, and 5 from Psalm 31: [movement 27]

In te, Domine, speravi, non confundar in aeternum: in iustitia tua libera me Inclina ad me aurem tuam, accelera ut eruas me, esto mihi in Deum protectorem et domum refugii, ut salvum me facias. In manus tuas commendo spiritum meum: redemisti me, Domine Deus veritatis.	In thee, O Lord, do I put my trust, let me never be ashamed; deliver me in thy righteousness. Bow down thine ear to me; deliver me speedily: be thou my strong rock, for an house of defence to save me. Into thine hand I commit my spirit. for thou hast redeemed me, O Lord God of truth.
	Psalm 31:1-2,5

49

It is interesting to note here the second appearance of the sixth word from the Cross ("Into thine hand I commit my spirit"). In this setting, the text is taken from Psalm 31:5 rather than Luke 23:46.

The *Lamentations of Jeremiah*, composed of five elegies lamenting the destruction of Jerusalem, is placed between Jeremiah and Ezekiel in the Septuagint, Vulgate and English Bible. The first four chapters consist of acrostics based on the Hebrew alphabet. Each verse of Chapters One and Two commences with a word whose initial consonant is successively one of the 22 letters of the Hebrew alphabet. A slight variation of the regular order occurs in Chapters three and four. The fifth Chapter is not an acrostic, although like the others it contains 22 stanzas. It is a prayer rather than an elegy.

Penderecki uses this short text twice in the *St. Luke Passion*. The portion of the text which he places after the Arrest of Jesus (Scene 2) and the Mocking of the High Priest (Scene 4) is taken from the version which appears in the Roman *Missal*. [movements 6 and 11]

Ierusalem, Ierusalem convertere ad Dominum, Deum Tuum.

Jerusalem, Jerusalem be converted to thy God.

From the *Lamentations of Jeremiah*, according to the version of the *Missal*.

Non-Biblical Interpolations

In addition to the biblical text discussed above, Penderecki includes four other liturgical interpolations in the Passion: the Latin hymn, "Vexilla regis prodeunt," the *Improperia*, the hymn "Pange lingua," and the sequence "Stabat mater."

The work opens with the "Vexilla regis prodeunt," a Latin hymn by Venantius Fortunatus which dates from c. 610. The original hymn consisted of eight stanzas, the first four describing Christ's crucifixion and the second four devoted to the Cross itself. This hymn, which celebrates the mystery of Christ triumphant on the Cross, was modified for liturgical use; the second strophe was dropped and two new stanzas "O crux ave" and a doxology were added in place of the original 6th and 7th. Penderecki sets this sixth verse of the hymn as an introduction to the Gospel narrative. [movement 1]

O Crux ave, spes unica,
Hoc Passionis tempore
Piis adange gratiam,
Reisque dele crimina.
Te, fons salutis, Trinitas,
Collaudet omnis spiritus.

O Cross, our one reliance, hail.
So may thy power with us avail
To give new virtue to the saint,
And pardon to the penitent.
To Thee, eternal Three in One,
Let homage meet by all be done.

Hymn "Vexilla regis prodeunt"

The *Improperia* (Latin, *reproaches*) is proper to the Good Friday morning liturgy in the Roman Catholic rite. The text is based on verses 3-4 of the sixth Chapter of Michah and the *Trisagion* (the oldest form of the Sanctus, written in the Greek language) which follows as the refrain. The main thought in this passage is the sorrow of our Lord with His people, because of their rejection of the benefits He has bestowed upon them. The text was originally sung to well-known plainsong melodies, preserved in the *Graduale Romanum*. In the Penderecki Passion the *Trisagion* is spoken by the choir; each Greek phrase (*Hagios o Theos*) (Holy God) is answered antiphonally by the Latin translation (*Sanctus Deus*). [movement 16]

Popule meus, quid feci tibi?	*My people, what have I done to thee?*
Aut in quo contristavi te?	*or in what have I grieved thee?*
Responde mihi.	*Because I brought thee out of the*
Qui eduxi te de terra Aegypti:	*land of Egypt: thou has prepared*
parasti Crucem Salvatori tuo.	*a Cross for thy Saviour.*
Hagios o Theos.	*Holy God.*
Sanctus Deus.	*Holy and Strong God.*
Hagios ischyros.	*Holy and Immortal God,*
Sanctus fortis.	
Hagios athanatos, eleison himas.	
Sanctus immortalis, miserere nobis.	*have mercy on us.*

Because it is one of the most famous of the Passiontide hymns, the *Pange lingua* has been used in the Good Friday ceremony of the veneration of the Cross since the 9th century. The original text consisted of 10 stanzas, each having three lines of trochaic meter, a form once used in the marching songs of the Roman soldiers. The text briefly recounts Christ's earthly life, embedded in the history of the redemption, beginning with man's fall, and makes passing allusions to the instruments of the Passion. Christ's Cross appears as a tree of life, expecially selected for the glorious task of bearing Christ. The antiphon to the unveiling of the Cross, not part of the original hymn, picks up this same theme. [movement 18]

Crux fidelis, inter omnes	*Faithful Cross! Above all other,*
arbor una nobilis:	*One and only noble tree!*
nolla silva talem profert,	*None in foliage, none in blossom,*
fronde, flora, germine.	*None in fruit thy peer may be;*
Dulce lignum, dulces clavos,	*Sweetest wood and sweetest iron!*
dulce pondus sustinet.	*Sweetest weight is hung on thee.*
Ecce lignum Crucis,	*Behold the wood of the Cross*
in quo salus mundi pependit.	*on which the salvation of the world was hanged.*

> *1st and 2nd antiphon of the Hymn "Pange lingua" and the antiphon to the unveiling of the Cross*

The final non-Biblical textual interpolation in St. Luke is the sequence *Stabat mater*, one of the five sequences still used in the Roman liturgy today. It was not one of the four to survive the liturgical reforms of the Council of Trient, but was restored to the Mass in 1727. Variously attributed to St. Bonaventure, Jacopone da Todi, and even to Pope Innocent II, it is assigned today to the Feast of the Seven

Sorrows of the Blessed Virgin Mary (September 15). The rhyme scheme of the first couplet, AABCCB (in the Latin setting), is duplicated in each of the nine subsequent couplets. This sequence has been a favorite text of composers from the 16th century on, including Palestrina, Scarlatti, Pergolesi, Haydn, Schubert, Rossini, Verdi, Dvořak, etc. [movement 24]

Stabat mater dolorosa	*Stood the Mother, stood though*
Iuxta Crucem lacrimosa,	*sighing, / Tearful, neath the cross,*
Dum pendebat Filius.	*where dying / Hung her only Son*
	and Lord.
Quis est homo, qui non fleret	*Who the man his tears with-*
Matrem Christi si videret	*holdeth / On her martyrdom pro-*
In tanto supplicio?	*found?*
Eia, Mater, fons amoris	*Mother, fount of love the purest,*
Me sentire vim doloris	*All the anguish thou endurest,*
Fac, ut tecum lugeam.	*Make me feel to mourn with thee.*
Fac, ut ardeat cor meum	*Make my heart with ardour*
In amando Christum Deum,	*glowing, / In the love of Christ*
Ut sibi complaceam.	*still growing, / Unto him well-*
	pleasing be.
Christe, cum sit hinc exire	*Christ, where hence my spirit's*
	lifted,
Da per Matrem me venire	*Through thy Mother be I gifted,*
Ad palmam victoriae.	*With the palm of victory.*
Quando corpus morietur,	*When my mortal flesh here dieth,*
Fac, ut animae donetur	*Grant my soul in glory flieth*
Paradisi gloria.	*Swift to paradise with thee.*

From the sequence "Stabat mater"

The Drama Arranged by Scenes

As a guide to the study of this work the discussion in chapters four through six will follow a dramatic structure of twelve scenes. A synopsis of the dramatic sequence is given below.[5]

Part I

Scene I: The Introduction and Christ Alone in the Garden

Following an opening hymn, the baritone sings Christ's prayer in the garden. There is then a brief response by the chorus. A touching response by the soprano concludes the scene.

Scene II: The Taking of Jesus

Near the end of an extended orchestral interlude, the narrator continues the story. He is joined by the chorus which relates the approach of Judas. Christ's response to Judas is sung by the baritone. The scene closes with a choral Lament and Psalm.

Scene III: Peter's Denial

After a brief orchestral passage, the crowd describes the taking of Christ to the house of the High Priest and the maid's approach to Peter in the garden. The three accusations of and denials by Peter follow and the scene ends with Peter's Lament, sung by the bass.

Scene IV: The Mocking Before the High Priest

Near the end of a long orchestral section, the chorus enters with wild outbursts of nonsense syllables as the narration begins. The chorus mocks Christ, who responds; and two meditative sections follow, one by the soprano and the other a Psalm by the chorus.

Scene V: Jesus Before Pilate and Herod

A long orchestral section opens this scene and is joined near the end by the chorus humming long, sustained, sliding passages. Following the narration the crowd bursts forth to accuse Christ of "perverting the nation..." Pilate questions Christ, who answers and is then sent to Herod, who returns him to Pilate. Pilate again questions Christ and the first part of the Passion concludes with a second outburst of the crowd: "Crucify Him."

Part II

Scene VI: The Way of the Cross

A short choral Psalm opens the second part of the work. This is followed by a long passacaglia for chorus and orchestra which accompanies the procession to Calvary. In this section the text from the *Improperia* "my people, what have I done to thee? Answer me ..." dominates and is set in a number of different textures. The scene concludes with a spoken prayer for mercy.

Scene VII: The Crucifixion

An orchestral introduction leads to the narrator telling of the crucifixion. Three long responses for soprano solo and chorus follow on the text of the *Pange lingua*.

Scene VIII: "Father, forgive them"

The tenors of the chorus begin this scene by reciting the words, "and they divided his garments among them . . ." A long a cappella Psalm concludes the scene.

Scene IX: The Mocking of Christ on the Cross

The narrative from the gospel opens the scene. This is followed by a long section of mocking in the chorus. The scene ends with the chorus singing the text, "If thou be king of the Jews, save thyself."

Scene X: Jesus Between the Thieves

In this short scene the chorus carries the statement of the first thief. The answer from the other malefactor is heard in the bass. The scene concludes with the baritone singing the response of Christ: "Verily I say unto thee, today thou shalt be with me in paradise."

Scene XI: Mary at the Cross

Following a brief orchestral passage, the narrator introduces the scene, and Christ's words to His mother are heard. The chorus responds with the *Stabat mater.*

Scene XII: The Death of Christ and the Finale

After a short orchestral introduction the narrator enters with the words, "and about the sixth hour . . ." and describes the death of Christ. A child then enters with the words "It is finished." An orchestral interlude follows. The final section of the *Passion* consists of fragments of texts and their respective musical settings from elsewhere in the work. The children's choir then introduces the theme of the final chorus. The adult choir and the orchestra then join them for the concluding psalm.

1 Wolfram Schwinger, *Penderecki: Begegnungen, Lebensdaten, Werkkommentare*, (Stuttgart: Deutsche Verlagsanstalt, 1979): 44

2 *Ibid.*

3 The Longueval Passion is one of the early examples of the practice of combining the texts from the four Gospels. For further information, see Chapter II, p. 32.

4 This method of text usage in the Passion, where parallel passages from the Old Testament are substituted for the Gospel narrative, is original with Penderecki.

5 The basic idea of this scene synopsis is taken from an article by Joseph Flummerfelt entitled, "Passion According to St. Luke – Penderecki," *Choral Journal* 13 (April 1973): 6-7.

Chapter IV

AN OVERALL VIEW OF THE MUSIC

This chapter exlores general characteristics of the music of the *St. Luke Passion* and serves as a preparation for the detailed descriptions of the individual movements which follow in Chapter V. It begins with a discussion of vocal setting and techniques and instrumental setting and techniques, and then proceeds to some of the more general aspects of rhythm and pitch, especially in terms of the composer's innovations in notation. The final sections of the chapter are devoted to a discussion of musical sources for the Passion and a description of large formal elements.

Vocal setting

Penderecki uses three four-part mixed choruses in St. Luke and occasionally divides some of the voice parts into two parts or more. At one point, in the *Stabat mater* (no. 24), he divides each voice part into four parts, making a total of 48 voice parts. In addition to this triple chorus, a two-part boys chorus sings in movements, 1, 3, 12, 16, 22, 25 and 27. The composer is highly selective in the use of the chorus parts; he uses many different combinations of various voice parts in accordance with the demands of the text and the musical context.

The choruses play a variety of roles in the Passion. In some movements they sound the words of the *turba* (the multitude); at other points they accompany or echo the Gospel story as spoken by the Evangelist; and occasionally they take over the words of the Gospel narrative from the Evangelist. In one of the most effective moments of the Passion, the death of Christ (no. 25), the boys chorus sings Christ's words *consummatus est* ("It is finished"). The most significant musical use of the chorus occurs in the contemplative movements such as the a cappella Psalms and the *Stabat mater*, three of which have been published as separate choral works.[1]

Three vocal soloists are used in the Passion. The words of Christ are sung by the baritone. The bass sings the roles of Peter, Pilate and the second thief. The soprano sings the role of the woman in the scene of Peter's denial (no. 8) but is used principally for the contemplative arias.

In setting the text, Penderecki uses a great variety of techniques, some of which go beyond the traditional division of recitative and aria found in other operatic and choral music. Some of these techniques are listed below:

a. spoken – normal prose style, neither pitch nor rhythm indicated.

b. recited – approximate rhythm indicated, no pitch indicated

c. *Sprechstimme* – approximate rhythm and approximate pitch indicated

d. singing – definite pitch and rhythm indicated

Any of these techniques may be used in any of the following textures:

a. monophonic – one voice or voice part alone

b. polyphonic imitative – the same material simultaneously in two or more voices, entering at different times

c. polyphonic non-imitative – different material presented simultaneously in two or more voices

d. "distributed text" – this innovative technique is used frequently and effectively in the *Passion*. The individual syllables of a word are presented in the proper temporal succession but are distributed among several voice parts.

It could be said that this "distributed text" has inherent symbolism, representing the need for community. No single part has an intelligible text; the text becomes apparent only when all parts work together.

Examples of several text setting techniques in the Passion may be seen in Ex. 4-1.

Ex. 4-1a, Penderecki, *St. Luke Passion*, movement 16, mm. 92-95

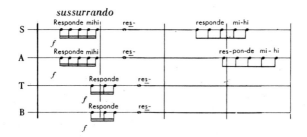

Ex. 4-1b, Penderecki, *St. Luke Passion*, movement 13, mm. 32-34

Ex. 4-1c, Penderecki, *St. Luke Passion*, movement 12, mm. 1-8

Occasionally Penderecki uses the voices, not to present text, but to produce instrumental sounds. Some of these are:

    a. *bocca chiuso* – singing with closed mouth (humming)
    b. imitating the sound of plucked strings (pizzicato)
    c. whistling
    d. singing on consonants only (percussive sounds)
    e. singing on vowels only (*Klangfarbenmelodie*) or tone color melody
    f. slides (glissandi)

Instrumental Setting

The instrumental setting of the Passion is exceptionally rich and varied, as can be seen from the roster of instruments given below:

4 flutes (fl)	gourd
bass clarinet in B-flat (bcl)	claves
2 alto saxophones (sxf)	4 cymbals (SATB)
3 bassoons (fg)	2 tam-tams (medium and bass)
contrabassoon (cfg)	2 gongs (chinese and javanese)

6 horns in F (cr)	bells (cmp)
4 trumpets in B-flat (tr)	vibraphone (vbf)
4 trombones (tn)	
tuba (tb)	harp (ap)
	pianoforte (pfte)
4 timpani (tmp)	harmonium (arm)
bass drum (gr c)	organ (org)
6 tom-toms (tomt)	
2 bongos (bg)	24 violins (vn)
snare drum (tmb mil.)	10 violas (vl)
whip (fr)	10 violoncellos (vc)
wood-blocks (bl di leg.)	8 doublebasses (vb)
rattle (rgn)	

A mere glance at this list will reveal that the orchestration is for the full "romantic" symphony orchestra; the only instruments not represented are the clarinets (except for bass clarinet) and the oboes and English horn. The string parts are frequently divided into many individual parts, sometimes with just one player to a part.

Penderecki is extremely selective and skillful in his use of this large apparatus. He never uses the entire orchestra together; indeed, he never calls for all the instruments in any given movement. In two movements, nos. 10 and 16, he uses the full family of wind, brass, and string instruments, but not the full complement of percussion and other instruments. Piano, organ, and harp are used quite sparingly: the piano is generally treated as a percussion instrument in keeping with the composer's belief that the tempered piano cannot blend well with orchestra instruments because it is always "out of tune."

Not only does Penderecki use a large number of different instruments, he also calls for a variety of types of articulation and methods of sound production from all the instrumental forces at his disposal. The following are some of the special effects used with string instruments:

harmonics (soft, flute-like sounds)

ponticello (playing near the bridge)

tremolo (rapidly repeated notes – indicated Z)

jarring sounds (indicated >>>>>>)

glissandi (slides)

playing between the bridge and the tail-piece (indicated ⫯⫯⫯)

The full range of dynamics and changes of dynamics is used.

Rhythm

Two types of rhythmic notation may be found in the Passion. A substantial portion of the work is written in traditional notation; indeed it is written in what might be called conservative traditional notation, with the quarter or eighth note as the basic duration or beat. The only time signatures used are $\frac{2}{4}$, $\frac{3}{4}$, $\frac{4}{4}$, $\frac{3}{8}$, $\frac{5}{8}$, $\frac{7}{8}$, and $\frac{9}{8}$. There are no compound meters in the work; the short section in $\frac{9}{8}$ does not have the compound meter division into beats with three divisions each. Some of the sections with traditional notation have no changes of meter; while others have frequent changes of meter. Penderecki tends to use traditional rhythmic notation for those sections in which the rhythmic aspects are relatively straight-forward and uncomplicated.

For more complex rhythmic passages Penderecki turns to a modern technique called "time-space" notation or "proportional" notation. Duration is indicated by the placement of the notehead within the bar. The shape of the notehead is merely suggestive and does not give precise duration information. In Ex. 4-2a only whole notes are used; the lines following the notes indicate that the note is to be sustained.

Ex. 4-2a, Penderecki, *St. Luke Passion*, Passacagalia, E

© 1968 by Hermann Moeck Verlag, Celle, West Germany.

In Ex. 4-2b, the use of thirty-second, sixteenth and eighth notes suggests the general speed of the notes but does not indicate the precise duration, only the placement of the notes within the measure and the relation of notes in one part to notes in another (see page 61).

Sections in which this type of notation is to be used, that is, sections in which the precise note values are not to be observed, are marked by this sign: $\curvearrowright$.

Two signs are used to indicate repetition:

· · · indicates the quickest possible repetition of the note

$\mathcal{Z}$ indicates a non-rhythmicized tremolo

In some instances the composer wishes to have a short passage repeated over and over. Rather than writing out all of these repetitions he uses the sign – – to indicate that the group of notes is to be repeated over and over as long as indicated.

Pitch

Penderecki's notation of pitch is also a mixture of tradition and innovation; indeed, he is credited with establishing some of the more significant innovations in modern pitch notation. The following special signs are used in the Passion:

highest pitch available on the instrument ⬆

lowest pitch available on the instrument ⬇

tone cluster (sound all the notes indicated on the line below the cluster for the duration of the solid black line).

The term "cluster" is used for any dense collection of notes built mostly in minor seconds, or quarter tones.

61

Ex. 4-2b, Penderecki, *St. Luke Passion,* 13 measures after ④

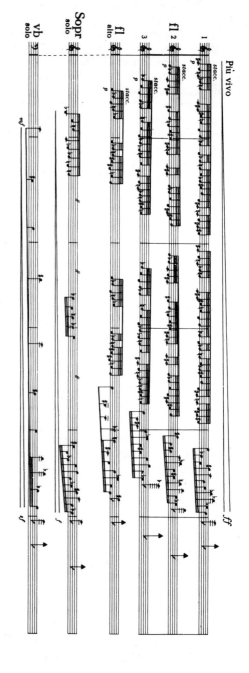

Penderecki indicates quarter tones with the following signs:

sharpen a quarter-tone ⌃

sharpen three quarter-tones ⧺

flatten a quarter-tone ♭

flatten three quarter-tones ⌐

In this work quarter tones are only used for strings or solo voices, not for chorus nor other instruments.

Details of Penderecki's use of pitch in melody and harmony will be given in Chapter VI. At this point, however, we shall introduce some special terms which may be used to describe certain common practices in Penderecki's music in general and the *Passion* in particular.

"Distributed melody." – This is a technique which calls for each successive note of the melody to be sounded by a different instrument or voice. Once the note has been sounded it is sustained so that at the end of the melodic line all of the notes of the melody are sounding simultaneously. Often this technique is used in conjunction with "distributed text" (see page 60).

"Flurry." – This term is used for a passage in which several parts are playing varied fast figures simultaneously. The passages may or may not be related, but the total effect is not one of contrapuntal lines, but rather a "cloud" of indistinguishable sound. Example 4-2b on Page 64, given to illustrate time-space notation, is also an example of a "flurry".

"Conjunct melody"	– melody that moves mostly by half and whole steps.
"Disjunct melody"	– melody that moves with some prominent wide leaps (usually larger than a sixth).
"Melisma"	– a passage in which one syllable is set to many notes.
"Free melodies"	– These are free in the sense that they are not directly related to important motives; they are not free in the sense of being improvised.
"Retrograde"	– means to play a melody or motive in reverse order, starting at the ending note of the original and moving backward to the first note.
"Inversion"	– means to play a melody "upside down", reversing the direction of each interval in the melody.
"Retrograde-inversion"	– is the combination of these two techniques.
"Expanded"	– means that one or more intervals of a melody is expanded.
"Varied"	– means that some other rearrangement of the original melody is used.

Two pre-existent melodies have been specifically identified by the composer as playing important roles in the musical substance of the Passion. The first of these is the so-called B A C H motive, a motive which was first used by J. S. Bach in the final uncompleted fugue from his monumental collection entitled *The Art of the Fugue*. This is a so-called *soggetto cavato* (carved-out subject) where a word or name is spelled with musical letters. In German musical notation, B stands for the note B-flat and H for the note B-natural. Ex. 4-3 shows the score of *The Art of the Fugue* at the point where the B A C H motive is used in counterpoint with a variant of the principal subject. J. S. Bach did not finish this work. His son C. Ph. E. Bach wrote at this point in the score the following words: "The composer died over this fugue [at the point] where the name B A C H is introduced in countersubject."

Ex. 4-3, J. S. Bach, *The Art of the Fugue.* B A C H motive

Penderecki has said that the B A C H motive is "the fundamental motive of the whole work, really the basic theme of leading motive (*Leitmotiv*), so to speak."[2] It appears in original form as well as in retrograde in many of the movements. See Chapter VI for a full discussion of the B A C H motive.

The second "borrowed" musical motive is derived from the Polish church song *Święty Boże* (Holy God). The composer has stated that this melody is the source for the opening four notes of the important melodic motive labelled Cantus Firmus I (CF-I) in the analysis in this book. This motive is sometimes called "Row I" because it is treated to some extent like a tone row in serial compositions. The designation "cantus firmus" is used because the composer in his discussions with the authors indicated his preference for the expression "Cantus firmus." "Cantus firmus" literally means "fixed song", but in music theory it usually designates a "pre-existent melody" which serves as the basis for a composition. This meaning seems appropriate for the way Penderecki uses the material in this work.

The derivation of the first four notes of Cantus Firmus I from the first phrase of *Święty Boże* is shown in Ex. 4-4a. Reversing the order of the two pairs of notes of this motive produces a motive which is labelled "*Święty Boże* - var" in the analysis. This motive figures prominently in no. 18. The derivation is shown in Ex. 4-4b; notice that this derivation is a "pair exchange," not a literal retrograde or backward version of the melody.

It is also possible to show relations between the hymn and two other important motives in the Passion, the "*Deus Meus*" motive and the "*Stabat mater*" motive.

These relations are shown in Ex. 4-4c; the Passion motives have been transposed to the same pitch level as the hymn to make the relations clear.

Ex. 4-4A, Derivation of *Cantus Firmus I* from *Święty Boże* Hymn. Phrase I

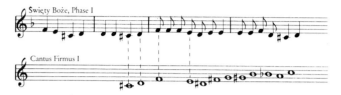

Ex. 4-4b, *Święty Boże* motive, reversed

Ex. 4-4c, Relations between *Święty Boże*, *Deus meus*, and *Stabat Mater* motives

Formal aspects

The overall division of the Passion into two large parts and 27 movements has already been discussed in Chapter III. The movements may be categorized accord-ing to musical type as follows:

Gospel Narratives, Evangelist and musical accompaniment, Nos. 2, 5, 8, 10, 13, 17, 19, 21, 22, 23, 25.

Gospel Narratives, Evangelist alone with no musical accompaniment, No. 15.

A cappella choruses, Nos. 7, 12, 20, 24.

Accompanied choruses, Nos. 1, 6, 14, 16, 27.
Solo arias, Nos. 4, 9, 11.
Solo arias with chorus, Nos. 3, 18.
Orchestra alone, No. 6.

The form of the individual movements is shaped primarily through the texts and in general does not conform strictly to any classical models such as *da capo aria, sonata-allegro* or others. Only one movement has been clearly designated formally and that is No. 16 which the composer has called a *passacaglia*. However, this term refers more to the compositional process of the work than to its sectional layout. Other movements fall more or less into sectional divisions. Probably the clearest is the five-part rondo like structure of movement 18. It is possible to find some type of two-part structure in nos. 9 and 20, three-part structure in nos. 8 and 12, and five-part structure in nos. 16 and 24. Other movements may have an over-all arch form. Details of formal structure are given in Chapter VI.

Another important aspect of macro or large formal structure is correspond-ences between movements created by obvious quoting of material from one movement in another movement. The four most obvious examples of this practice are:

No. 1, meas. 19-44 and No. 24, meas. 57-86	The music is almost identical except for slight changes made to accommodate the different text. The two texts both contain the word *fons* (fount)
No. 6 and No. 11	Both are based on the same text and have the same rhythmic motive
No. 14 and No. 20	No. 14 presents just verse 16 of Psalm 22, No. 20 repeats this text and music and then continues with verses 17-20
No. 18, meas. 7-29, 43-50 and No. 26 complete	The music is the same but in no. 26 the parts for solo soprano and alto flute are played by two sections of violas.

Another contributing factor to the unity of Part I of the Passion is considerable emphasis on the pitch G. This pitch is prominent in movements 1, 3, 4, 6, 10, and 11, and at the end of movement 13.

In Part II, no single pitch is emphasized as strongly; however, the work closes on an E major chord that somehow seems logical, almost inevitable. One explana-tion for this can be found in the "Domine" motive which figures so prominently in the work. This motive usually resolves to an E-minor chord. The E-major chord at the conclusion can be regarded as the same chord with a Picardy third. Penderecki confirms this in the following quotation from an interview in 1977:

> ... the only resolution of "Domine" is at the end of the piece. The children are singing "Domine, Deus" at a fast rate, which is the only resolution of the chord. Release! The whole piece is preparing this chord.[3]

[1] The *Stabat Mater* and two choruses from the St. Luke, *In Pulverem Mortis* and *Miserere* are published separately. The information for these publications is listed below:

    Stabat Mater (Latin) – for three mixed choruses; published in America by Belwin-Mills (Melville, NY., 1971). Published in Poland by Polskie Wydawnictwo Muzyczne (Krakowskie Przedmiescie 7, Warsaw, Poland).

    Two Choruses from *The Passion According to St. Luke* (latin) – score published by Hermann Moeck Verlag, Celle, West Germany (American agent: European American Music) contains: *In Pulverem Mortis* – for three part mixed chorus a cappella; *Miserere* – for three part mixed chorus and optional Jr. chorus, a cappella. These two works are also available separately.

[2] From a televised interview with Ludwik Erhard, ZDF (second German Television Network) 20/5/70.

[3] David Felder and Mark Schneider, "An Interview with Krzysztof Penderecki," *The Composer* 8 (1976-1977):17.

Chapter V

A DESCRIPTION OF THE INDIVIDUAL MOVEMENTS

This chapter begins with a table of the important musical motives. Each motive is given a name based on its source or its accompanying text and also a number for ease of reference (Table I). When one motive is based on another this relationship will be indicated by such abbreviations as inv. (inversion), retro. (retrograde), retro-inv. (retrograde-inversion), exp. (expansion) or var. (variant). (See the preceding chapter for a full explanation of these terms.)

Motives in the Penderecki *Passion*, in contrast to typical motives in earlier music, are usually characterized by their pitch content rather than their rhythmic content. For this reason they are cited in whole notes with no rhythm indicated. In some cases, however, rhythm does play a significant role and is shown for the particular motive. In one motive, the "Domine" motive (No. 9), the harmony is important so the accompanying voices are shown as well.

In the outline descriptions, the first column (M) shows the measure number. Except for the *Stabat mater* (no. 24) measure numbers are not given in the score, and therefore they would have to be added to the score by hand for those wishing to use the guide for detailed score study. The second column is devoted to the text, including a literal, word by word English translation. The third column indicates the vocal and/or instrumental setting and the fourth column cites the important motives and briefly describes the text setting, texture, and other points of musical interest. Not every detail of every section is given, but it is hoped that sufficient information is provided in a clear enough form to allow the reader to follow the outline while listening. For some movements, such as No. 8, events move at such a rapid pace that it would be necessary to study the outline in advance of listening. Abbreviations for instruments and terms used to describe special musical characteristics are those given in Chapter IV. In some instances it is virtually impossible to follow the text by listening because of the complexity of the texture or the type of text setting technique being used. These events are labelled ?text?. Events with no text are marked – – – in the Text column. Events which continue through the following events are marked $\downarrow_{16}^{15}$.

Table I

Table of Motives in Penderecki's *St. Luke Passion*

27 BACH-row

28 Święty-Boże-var.

29 Crux

30 Święty-Boże-var.-exp.

31 In-pulverem-inv.-retro

32 In-pulverem-retro

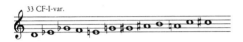

33 CF-I-var.

34 In te

35 Non confundar

71

PART I

1. *O Crux*	"Oh, Cross"	Acommpanied chorus Text: Hymn "Vexilla Regis Prodeunt" 21-26

M	Text	Voices, Instruments	Musical Materials
1	Crux	full chorus, org., tmp.	short, four-octave G
2	Ave	boys	sigh (1)
3	O, Crux	full chorus	short, four-octave G
4		low winds, brass and strings	Cantus firmus-I (CF-1) (2) distributed-sustained
6	Crux	full chorus org., low brass	12-note chord built in fourths
7	Crux ave	boys sop.	Cantus firmus-II (CF-II) (3)
		org.	BACH – retro (4)
8	Crux ave	I alto, boys sop.	BACH (5)
9	Spes	I tenor	CF-I (2)
10	unica	I alto	sigh (1)
11	O Crux	full chorus, brass	four-octave D with staggered entries and varied dynamics, ending with glissando
13	ave	boys	sigh (1)
15	spes	altos, tenors	cluster with staggered entries
16	unica	sop.	repeated A
17	Hoc Passionis tempore	tenors, basses	varied conjunct figures in imitation
18	Piis adauge gratiam Reisque dele crimina	sop., alto	recited
19	Te fons salutis, Trinitas, collaudet omnis spiritus	full chorus	long contrapuntal section based on *Stabat mater* (6) and sigh (1) motives. Builds gradually from two to fourteen parts. Pedal A
37		org., vb.	
44	Crux	full chorus	short, five-octave A
45		vb.	CF-I (2)

M	Text	Voices, Instruments	Musical Materials
46		org.	BACH-retro (4)
47	?text? Crux/ave	full chorus	Sigh (1) and Sigh-inv. (7) simultaneously on all 12 pitches in varied rhythms, ending with glissando

In this powerful introductory movement Penderecki captures conflicting emotions of struggle and victory, of despair and hope, of supplication and confidence. The recurring cries of *Crux* divide the work sectionally. The fact that their intervallic relations are all perfect fifths might suggest classical tonal relations. This is in contrast to the avoidance of classical tonal relations in the melodic materials themselves.

The two primary musical sources, BACH and *Święty Boże* are introduced immediately in the movement. The "sigh" motive is so-called from the tradition of Baroque music where such descending halfstep motives were often used to depict sorrow. The *Stabat mater* motive is named because it appears in the a cappella chorus, *Stabat mater*, the first movement of the Passion to be written.

2	*Et egressus*	"And he went out"	Gospel narrative (Jesus on the Mount of Olives) Text: St. Luke 22:39-44

M	Text	Voices, Instruments	Musical Materials
1	- - -	tmp, org. vb. Evangelist	pedal (sustained) A spoken

Et egressus ibat secundum consuetudinem in montem Olivarum.
Secuti sunt autem illum et discipuli . . . positis genibus orabat dicens:

2	Pater si vis, Pater transfer calicem istum a me. Pater, verumtamen non mea voluntas, sed Tua fiat.	baritone (Jesus)	Melodic line begins with sigh-inv (7) and then is a free melody using a mixture of very small and very large intervals, reaching a climax at the end on a high A.
↓			
9		low strings	short accompanying passage of free conjunct melody

The freely melismatic and highly expressive line effectively portrays the supplication and acceptance of Jesus. Structure is provided by the use of the "Sigh-inv." motive on the word *Pater* at the beginning of each phrase. This motive also ends the movement.

3	*Deus meus*	"My God, My God"	Aria for baritone
			Text: Psalm 22: 1-2
			Psalm 5:1

M	Text	Voices, Instruments	Musical Materials
1	Deus meus, respice in me quare me derelinquisti	baritone (Jesus) org. harm, low str.	Deus meus motive (8), then free disjunct melodic material
12	Domine	boys, tenors	Domine (9)
13	Deus meus	baritone (Jesus)	Deus meus (8)
15	– – –	chorus men	Deus meus-inv. (10) on vowels
20	Verba mea auribus, percipe	chorus men	Sigh(1), distributed-sustained
22	Deus, meus	baritone (Jesus)	Deus meus (8)
23	Verba mea auribus	boys, tenor	Sigh (1)
28	Domine	full chorus	Domine (9)
30	Intellige clamorem meum	chorus men	Emphatic even eighth notes starting from a central E-flat and moving out in half steps to build a twelve tone chord, ending with a glissando
33	Deus meus	baritone (Jesus)	Deus meus (8)
34	Deus meus	full chorus	Deus meus (8) and Deus-meus-inv. (10) in imitation on various pitch levels, thick contrapuntal texture.
41	clamabo	full chorus	Sigh (1) in 12-note chords
43	Deus meus	baritone (Jesus)	Deus meus (8)
46	clamabo per diem ed non exaudies	baritone	free melody
51	intellige clamorem meum	altos, tenors, basses	descending lines (steps and half steps)
57	Deus meus	baritone (Jesus)	Deus meus (8)

One of the most immediatelly accessible movements in the Passion, this work is also one of the most tightly unified. The "Deus meus" motive appears over twenty times and the "Deus-meus-inv." is also used frequently in counterpoint with it. Contrast is provided by the settings of the other words of the text; structural division is created by the recurring "Domine" motives. This comes as close as any movement in the Passion to being clearly in a single key at the beginning and end, namely G minor. The work has a highly-controlled arch of tension, building to a climax at the outcry "clamabo" in measure 39, and then subsiding thereafter.

4.	*Domine, quis habitabit in tabernaculo Tuo?*	"Lord, who shall abide in thy tabernacle?"	Aria for soprano Text: Psalm 15,1: 4-8; 16,9

M	Text	Voices, Instruments	Musical Materials
1	Domine	boys, tenors,	Domine (9)
2	– – –	soprano solo	"Klangfarbenmelodie," humming and then vowels O E A I
3	– – –	fl, arm, vb	unisons and then clusters
8	– – –	vb	flurries
9	– – –	soprano	melismas
13	– – –	flutes	flurries ending on highest notes
19		flutes	cluster glissando
	Domine, quis habitabit in tabernaculo Tuo	soprano solo	Sigh (1) with quarter tones
24	– – –	fl. arm	cluster
	Domine	soprano solo	Sigh (1), quarter tones
25		cmp, tr	high loud cluster and then wide ranging free melody in solo trumpet
	aut quis requiescet	soprano solo	free melody with wide leaps, ends with Sigh-inv (7)
29	in monte sancto tuo	soprano solo	slow quarter tone trill
		alto flute	undulating sound
30		low brass	low chords
31	in pace dormiam et caro mea requiescet in spe	soprano solo	repeated notes, melismas and Sigh (1) motives
34		flutes, vb	cluster

75

The quiet mood of this movement is established through an emphasis on tone color rather than melody at the beginning. The one outcry in the middle, heralded by the bell and trumpet cluster, is all the more shocking because of the quiet passage which precedes it. The quarter tone writing in this movement is especially effective. The quarter tones are always approached by step, giving them the effect of intensified "sigh" motives.

5.	*Adhuc eo loquente*	"And while he yet *spake*"	Gospel narrative (The Taking of Jesus Text: St. Luke 22:47-53
M	*Text*	*Voices, Instruments*	*Musical Materials*
1		brass	cluster with varied crescendos and sFFp accents
7		vc, vb	cluster with varied attacks, ending with glissando to highest notes
19		brass	clusters, tremolo
23		vn, vl	cluster, muted, vibrato
24		fl, fg	cluster, tremolo
26		vc, vb	cluster, all rapid down bows, rough sound
27		brass	cluster, crescendo
28		percussion	flurry
29		vc, vb	cluster, all rapid down bows
30		brass	cluster, crescendo
31		organ, strings	loud, wide cluster
32		basses, tmp, tomt vb	moderately fast flurry short notes pizzicato (quasi-pizzicato in voices)
34	Adhuc eo loquente ecce turba, et qui vocabatur	Evangelist	spoken
35	Iudas unus de duodecim	full chorus tenors	recited together spoken one after the other
36	et appropinquavit Iesu ut oscularetur eum ?text?	full chorus	*Sprechstimme* in canon, phrases repeated over and over ending on highest notes

M	Text	Voices, Instruments	Musical Materials
37	Iuda, osculo Filium hominis tradis?	baritone (Jesus)	spoken
38	Quasi ad latronem existis cum gladiis et fustibus? Sed haec est hora vestra et potestas tenebrarum.	baritone (Jesus)	sung, free melody emphasizing alternation of half steps and wide leaps
		vc, vb, clb, cfg	free conjunct lines

The extensive orchestra introduction effectively prepares the listener for the drama of the betrayal of Jesus by Judas. The "clusters" and "flurries" in measures 1 through 34 all overlap one another so that the aural effect is one of a kaleidoscope of shifting orchestral colors.

An interesting effect is achieved when the chorus anticipates the words of the Evangelist (*unus de duodecim*) and then takes over the Evangelist's role in narrating the Biblical story. Jesus responds to the betrayal by Judas, first with speaking and then with singing. With such a wide variety of text setting techniques at his disposal, Penderecki is able to seek out the one that will best illuminate the meaning and emotion of a given text.

6.	*Ierusalem*	"Jerusalem"	Accompanied chorus Text: *Lamentations of Jeremiah* according to the version of the *Missal*

M	Text	Voices, Instruments	Musical Materials
1		cmp, org, tn, tb	pedal G
	Ierusalem	sop, alto, bass	Jerusalem (11) G octave
3	Ierusalem	tenor (6-part)	Jerusalem (11) cluster
5	convertere	sop, alto, tenor	Jerusalem (11) G octave
7	ad Dominum	full chorus	G octave, varied rhythms
8	Deum Tuum	bass (6-part)	Sigh (1), Sigh-inv (7) imitation
14		clb, fg, org, tamt	low cluster built note by note

The "Jerusalem" motive is primarily rhythmic. It recurs in movements 11 with different pitches.

77

7.	*Ut quid Domine*	"Why standest thou afar off, O Lord?"	A capella chorus Text: Psalm 10:1

M	Text	Voices, Instruments	Musical Materials
1	Ut quid Domine recessisti longe	chorus I	CF-1 (2), BACH-var (12) CF-I-inv (13), Sigh (1)
15	Domine	full chorus	Domine (9)

The distance mentioned in the text is effectively captured in the soft dynamics of the movement. The unity of the movement comes from the similarity of the melodic gestures. The "Domine" motive provides a link to earlier movements and makes an effective close.

8.	*Comprehendentes*	"They took him"	Gospel narrative (Peter's denial) Text: St. Luke 22:54-62

M	Text	Voices, Instruments	Musical Materials
1		gng, cmp, arm, pfte	two long low tritones
3		arm, fl, vl	soft clusters
6	?text? Comprehendentes autem eum duxerunt ad domum principis sacerdotum. Quem cum vidisset ancilla quaedam sedentem ad lumen, et eum fuisset intuita, dixit	tenor (9 part)	recited on repeated notes, varied entries
		fl, vbf, vl	flurries
8	Et hic	solo soprano	tritone leap
		chorus sopranos	leaps of various intervals to notes forming clusters around soprano cluster
	cum illo erat	solo soprano	free disjunct melody
9	Mulier non novi illum	bass (Peter)	free disjunct melody
11		sxf, tr	legato flurries
12		cr, tn, tb	accented rhythmic chords

M	Text	Voices, Instruments	Musical Materials
↓		arm, vl, gng	cluster
13	Et post posillum alius videns eum dixit	Evangelist	spoken
14	Et tu	basses	Sigh (1), Sigh-inv (7)
15	de illis es	altos, tenors	cluster, syncopated repeated notes
16	O homo non sum	bass (Peter)	free disjunct melody
18		tamt, gng, arm, cr, tr	cluster
↓	Et intervallo facto quasi horae unius, alius quidam affirm-abat dicens:	Evangelist	spoken
	?text? Vere et hic cum illo erat	full chorus	recited at different times
19	Nam et Galilaeus est	full chorus	recited together
20	Homo, nescio, quid	bass (Peter)	two tritones and then Sigh (1)
22		chorus, women vb	cluster built up note by note ending with glissando
↓		org	CF-II
23	Et continuo adhuc illo loquente canta-vit gallus. Et conver-sus Dominus respexit Petrum. Et recordatus est Petrus verbi Domini. Et egressus foras flevit amare.	Evangelist	spoken

Penderecki has set the events of this movement at a very rapid pace. The three-fold denial of Peter dictates the structure of this compact but powerful movement. The tritone, ancient musical symbol for the Devil and the tragic, permeates the movement from the opening two chords to the final solo of Peter.

9.	*Iudica me*	"Judge me"	Aria Text: Psalm 43:1
M	Text	Voices, Instruments	Musical Materials
1	Iudica me	Bass (Peter)	Judica me (14)
3	Deus	Bass (Peter)	Sigh (1)
4	et discerne causam meam	Bass (Peter)	free conjunct melody

M	Text	Voices, Instruments	Musical Materials
6		clb, cfg	Free melody with minor thirds and ninths prominent
9	Iudica me, Deus et discerne causam meam	bass (Peter)	similar to m. 1-5

The brevity of this short setting of a single Psalm verse still allows for a full expression of Peter's remorse. It is clearly in two parts separated by an instrumental interlude.

10.	*Et viri, qui tenebant illum*	"And the men that held Jesus mocked him"	Gospel narrative (The mocking before the high priest) Text: St. Luke 22:63-79

M	Text	Voices, Instruments	Musical Materials
1		muted strings	flurries, instruments enter one at a time
21		winds	legato flurries
31		brass	flurries
37		fl, cfg, vb	flurries
41		percussion	flurries
43		strings	flurries
50		chorus	flurry, rapidly repeated consonant P, starting on highest note and descending to lowest note
		percussion	flurry
52		basses	flurry, consonant T
		clb, sxf, fg	flurry
53		chorus	flurry, consonant T
		percussion vc, vb	flurries, strings play behind bridge, coarse squeaky sounds
	Et viri, qui tenebant illum, illudebant ei caedentes. Et velaverunt eum et percutiebant faciem eius et interrogabant eum dicentes:	Evangelist	spoken

M	Text	Voices, Instruments	Musical Materials
56	⌐	chorus	flurry, consonant P mocking laughter ending with highest notes and whistles
↓	⌐	cr, tr	flurries
58		vbf, arm, vn	cluster
59	Prophetiza	chorus	recited together
		percussion, vb	flurry
60	quis est	chorus	recited at various times
61	qui te percussit	chorus	recited together
62	?text? Tu ergo es Filius Dei	chorus	distributed sustained melody (cluster)
65	Vos dicitis, quia ergo sum	baritone (Jesus)	free melody, ends with sigh-inv (7)
		organ	free slow conjunct melody

Again, as in No. 5, the agitated orchestra introduction effectively prepares for the drama that follows. The movement reaches a powerful climax in measure 55, followed by the mocking of the crowd and the reply of Jesus.

11.	*Ierusalem*	"Jerusalem"	Lamento (Aria) Text: *Lamentations of Jeremiah* in the version of the *Missal*

M	Text	Voices, Instruments	Musical Materials
1		cmp, vn, vb	cluster
2	Ierusalem	soprano solo	Jerusalem-var (15)
5	Con-	soprano solo	melisma
6	-vertere	soprano solo	high repeated notes
		cr, tr	loud cluster
7	ad Dominum	soprano solo	free low conjunct melody

This quiet movement follows the turbulence of movement 10 just as no. 6 followed no. 5. The text is the same as no. 6 and the rhythm of the "Jerusalem" motive returns.

12.	*Miserere*	"Be merciful"	A cappella Psalm Text: Psalm 56:1

M	Text	Voices, Instruments	Musical Materials
1	Miserere	basses	BACH-retro (4) distributed-sustained
6	Miserere	tenors	BACH (5)
9	Miserere mei	altos	CF-II (3)
13 ↓	Deus	boys	repeated C
14 ↓	miserere	basses	BACH-retro (4)
15	miserere	boys	BACH (5)
18	miserere	tenors	Święty Boże (16)
21 ⌐	conculcavit me homo	altos	CF-II-inv (17)
└	miserere	I bass	CF-II (3)
24 ⌐	Miserere	II tenor	CF-II (3)
└	Miserere	II bass	CF-II-retro (18)
29	?text? tota de impugnans tribulavit me	chorus	12 tone chord built up with one note at a time, distributed syllables
35	Miserere mei Deus	basses	Miserere (19)
40 ↓	quoniam	I tenors	CF-II retro (18)
41	Miserere	I tenor	CF-II-retro-inv (20)
43 ⌐	conculcavit me homo	I alto	CF-II-inv (17)
└	conculcavit me homo	II alto	CF-II (3)
46	Miserere mei	III alto	CF-II (first 6 notes) (3)
	Miserere	III bass	BACH (5)
48	Miserere	boys, tenors,	cluster, distributed-sustained, ending on low A alone

This movement has been called the heart (*Herzstück*, Wolfram Schwinger) of the *Passion*; certainly it is one of the most moving and effective. Textually and texturally it may be divided into three parts (1-28, 29-45 and 46-53). It has great unity derived from the use of a limited number of motives. Even the motive labelled *Miserere* (19) is similar in structure to the CF-II and the BACH motives.

13.	*Et surgens omnis multitudo*	"And the whole multitude of them arose"	Gospel narrative (Jesus before Pilate) Text: St. Luke 23: 1-22

M	Text	Voices, Instruments	Musical Materials
1		vn, org, arm	cluster of highest notes
4		vc, vb, vl	quarter-tone cluster starting from middle notes and adding notes above and below
7		fl, sxf, fg, cr	cluster, same technique
8		pfte, org, perc	isolated strokes or notes
10		chorus	humming varied slow moving contrapuntal lines ending on lowest note cluster in altos
12		brass	cluster
13	Et surgens omnis multitudo eorum duxerunt illum ad Pilatum. Coeperunt autem illum accusare dicentes:	Evangelist	spoken
14	Hunc	chorus	spoken together
	↓	brass	cluster with repeated and sustained notes
18	in – Hunc	chorus	spoken, glissando to highest notes
20 ↓		percussion, vc, vb	flurries, including notes played behind the bridge
21	?text? invenimus subvertentem gentem nostram et prohibentem tributa dare Caesari et dicentem se	chorus	spoken distributed text, freely repeated phrases
28	Christum regem esse.	chorus	spoken together
		brass	cluster
30	Tu es rex Iudaeorum?	bass (Pilate)	CF-I (2) first 5 notes then *Sprechstimme*
33	Tu dicis	baritone (Jesus)	Deus-meus var. (21)
34	Domine	chorus	domine (9)

M	Text	Voices, Instruments	Musical Materials
36		org, vb	Deus meus-inv (22)
37 ↓	Nihil invenio causae	bass (Pilate)	free melody with half-steps and wide leaps
39		tn	descending stepwise line
42		brass	cluster lowest notes
	Et remisit eum ad Herodem	Evangelist	spoken
43	Herodes autem interrogabat illum multis sermonibus	chorus	recited together
		org, vn	quarter-tone cluster
44	At ipse nihil illi respondebat	chorus	spoken
		perc	isolated notes and strokes
47	Sprevit autem illum Herodes et indutum veste alba. Remisit ad Pilatum. Pilatus autem convocatis principibus sacerdotum.	tenors	recited in canon
		sop, alto	cluster built note by note
53	Ecce nihil dignum morte actum est ei. Emendatum ergo illum dimittam	bass (Pilate)	free melody with half-steps and leaps
		vc, vb	pedal A
58		tn, tb	Sigh (1), Sigh-inv (7)
62	?text? Tolle hunc	chorus	spoken together
	et dimitte nobis	chorus	spoken at different times
	Barabbam	chorus	spoken together
64		tn, tb, org, vc, vb	cluster with glissando at end
	Iterum autem Pilatus locutus est ad eos volens dimittere Iesum. At illi succlamabant dicentes:	Evangelist	spoken
65	Crucifige illum	chorus	sung together on octave D in rhythm
66	Quid enim mali fecit iste?	bass (Pilate)	free melody with half-steps and wide leaps

M	Text	Voices, Instruments	Musical Materials
71	Crucifige illum	chorus	sung in rhythm first on unison G, then on 5-note chord, finally on 12-note chord made up of 3 diminished sevenths a half step apart.
72		brass, org, vc, vb	cluster

This is the third of five movements in which the orchestra plays a leading role in conveying the excitement of the Passion drama. The text for this movement is the longest of all the movements, but Penderecki sets it in a compact, effective manner. The movement builds towards a climax at the very end, and this provides an effective ending for the entire first part. One of the most subtle touches is the subtle reference to the "Deus meus" motive (8). These portray Christ's despair without having Him give verbal expression to it.

Part II

14.	*In pulverem mortis*	"Thou hast brought me into the dust of death"	Accompanied chorus

M	Text	Voices, Instruments	Musical Materials
1	In pulverem mortis	I alto	in pulverem (23)
	deduxisti me	II alto	in pulverem-inv (24)
2		gng, tamt, org, vc, vb	pedal D and isolated strokes
3	deduxisti me	tenors, basses	octave D, distributed text

The second part of the *Passion* is opened with this brief setting of one verse of Psalm 22.

15.	*Et baiulans*	"And bearing the Cross"	Gospel narrative (The Way of the Corss) Text: St. John 19: 17

M	Text	Voices, Instruments	Musical Materials
	Et baiulans sibi crucem exivit in eum, qui dicitur Calvariae, locum Hebraice autem Golgotha.	Evangelist	spoken

This is the only "movement" of the Passion with spoken text alone. It is a "movement" only in the sense that it represents a change of Biblical scene.

16.	*Popule meus*	"My people"	Passacaglia (accompanied chorus) Text: Improperia

M	Text	Voices, Instruments	*Musical Materials*
1		tmp	BACH-retro (4)
3	?text? Popule meus	altos	BACH-orn (25), distributed-sustained melody, distributed text
9	Popule meus	basses	BACH-orn (25), sustained-distributed melody, distributed text
16	Popule meus	altos, tenors	BACH-orn (25), sustained-distributed melody, distributed text
26	Popule meus	I tenor	CF-II (3)
	Quid feci tibi	basses	BACH-orn (25), sustained-distributed melody, distributed text
27	quid feci tibi	II tenor	CF-II-var (26)
34	Popule meus	boys	BACH-orn (25)
	quid feci tibi	altos, tenors	CF-II-retro (18), sustained-distributed melody, distributed text
47	Popule meus	boy soprano	CF-II (3)
	quid feci tibi	boy alto	BACH-orn (25)
	Popule meus	basses	CF-I (2) (notes 2-5)
57	Popule meus	full chorus	Melodic material for this dense contrapuntal section is based on different versions of CF-I and CF-II. The section starts slowly in I tenor and then adds voices and increases speed and dynamics
66	Aut in quo contristavi te	Chorus I, II	CF-II (3), sustained-distributed melody, distributed text
		brass	cluster, note by note
68	Popule meus	Chorus III	BACH-orn (25)
73	Responde mihi	Chorus	Sigh (1), Sigh-inv (7)
80		tmp	BACH (5)

M	Text	Voices, Instruments	Musical Materials
86		tamt	two isolated strokes
88		vn, vl, arm, fl	cluster, quarter-tone
92 ↓ 97	Responde mihi aut in quo contristavi te	chorus	recited, various rhythms
		winds, brass	flurries
111	Responde	chorus	recited, together
		brass, org, perc	cluster
120	Popule meus	basses	BACH (5) sustained-distributed
129 ↓	Popule meus	altos	BACH-retro (4) sustained-distributed
131	Popule meus quid feci tibi	sopranos	Święty Boże (16) divided
136	quid feci tibi	tenors	Sigh (1)
142		winds	cluster
145		chorus	whistling glissando
146		arm, vn, vl ·	cluster (harmonics, whistling, flute like sounds)
152		vb, vc, vl	BACH-row (27) in canon
168	?text? Popule meus	full chorus	Sigh (1) and Sigh-inv (7) on all twelve pitches
174	?text? Quia eduxi te de	I tenor I II	various motives in counterpoint, distributed text
		II tenor I II	
	terra Aegypti	III tenor I	BACH-retro (4)
		III tenor II	BACH (5)
		arm	cluster
		vl, vc	slow motives in counter-point
183 ↓	popule meus	boys, sopranos, tenors	slow motives
185 ↓	quia eduxi te de terra Aegypti	altos, basses	faster motives, repeated over and over
196 ↓	quid feci tibi	boys	BACH-retro (4) ornamented
200	responde mihi	Chorus III	spoken
202	?text? quia eduxi te de terra Aegypti	tenors, basses vc, vb	cluster, differing attacks

M	Text	Voices, Instruments	Musical Materials
211	Popule meus	boys	CF-I (2)
	?text? parasti Crucem Salvatori	Chorus I, II	CF-II-var (26) sustained-distributed melody, distributed text
	Salvatori	Chorus III	BACH (5)
		org	BACH (5)
		cr	CF-II (3)
217	Crucem	boys	octave A-flat
	Salvatori	sopranos	cluster, repeated notes
		low winds, brass strings	BACH (5) and cluster
221	Hagios o Theos Sanctus Deus Hagios ischyros Sanctus fortis Hagios athanatos, eleison himas	chorus	spoken antiphonally

Willi Apel has defined a *passacaglia* as "a continuous variation based on a clearly distinguishable ostinato which normally appears in the bass but which may also be transferred occasionally to an upper part." The ostinato or repeated melody in this case is the "BACH" motive or its variant, the "BACH-retro" motive. Together these motives completely saturate the movement, being heard over 100 times in various presentations. The other motives form a virtual compendium of the entire material from the whole Passion. It should be remembered that this movement was the first new movement (after the *Stabat mater*) to be written expressly for the Passion. The movement may be divided as follows, taking text and texture into consideration:

  1-65:   Popule meus, quid feci tibi

 66-116: Aut in quo contristavi te. Responde mihi

117-181: Popule meus, quid feci tibi. Quia eduxi te de terra Aegypti

182-219: Popule meus, quid feci tibi. Quia eduxi te de terra Aegypti parasti Crucem Salvatori tuo.

220- .   Hagios o Theos. Sanctus Deus. Hagios ischyros. Sanctus fortis. Hagios athanatos, eleison himas. Sanctus immortalis, miserere nobis.

Notice how the first four sections each repeat some text of the preceding section(s) and then add the new text, thus keeping the central ideas of the text present for the listener at all times.

One of the most fascinating aspects of this seminal work for the Passion is the way in which it moves between sections in which the text may be easily understood and sections in which it may not be clearly perceived, or between sections in which the melodic material stands out in clear relief and sections in which it is concealed in a dense contrapuntal texture.

Instruments are used somewhat sparingly in the movement, but the number of different vocal texture and timbres provides a sense of variety to the work.

17.	*Ibi crucifixerunt eum*	"Then they crucified him"	Gospel narrative (The crucifixion) Text: St. Luke: 23:33
M	*Text*	*Voices, Instruments*	*Musical Materials*
1		brass and organ	two clusters separated by pauses
5		strings	BACH-row (27) in imitation starting in cellos and moving through all strings
37		brass and organ	cluster
	Ibi crucifixerunt eum et latrones, unum a dextris et alterum a sinistris	Evangelist	spoken

This movement seems to confirm the symbolism of the BACH motive. The motive has been described by German musicologists for many years as one of the "cross" motives, because the melodic direction of the notes spatially describes the shape of a cross.

18.	*Crux fidelis*	"Faithful cross"	Aria with chorus Text: 1st and 2nd antiphon of the hymn *Pange Lingua* and the antiphon to the unveiling of the Cross
M	*Text*	*Voices, Instruments*	*Musical Materials*
1		solo viola	Święty Boże-var. (28)
3		vl, timp	Święty Boże-var. (28) distributed-sustained melody
9		vc	Crux (29) and continued legato line
11	Crux	solo soprano	Sigh (1)
17		fl alto	Sigh-inv. (7), Sigh (1)
30	Crux fidelis inter omnes arbor una nobilis	solo soprano	Crux (29) and continued line
55	Ecce lignum Crucis	sop, altos	octave E repeated

M	Text	Voices, Instruments	Musical Materials
58 ↓	in quo salus mundi pependit	sop, altos	Święty Boże-var-exp (30) distributed-sustained melody and text
59	Dulce lignum	soprano solo vc, vb pizz.	Sigh (1) "chordal" figures
68 ↓		vc	Święty Boże-var-exp (30) distributed-sustained
72		vb	Crux (29)
75 ↓		vc, vb	Crux (29)
77 ↓		fl alto	Sigh (1)
82	Crux fidelis nulla silva talem profert, fronde, germine	solo soprano	long lines based on Sigh (1) and Crux (29)
99	Ecce lignum crucis	womens voices	Święty Boże-var-exp (30) distributed-sustained
101		vl, vc	Święty Boże-var-exp (30) distributed-sustained
102		vb	Sigh motives
108 ↓		vc, vb	long legato lines based on Sigh (1) and Crux (29)
127 ↓	dulce pondus sustinet	soprano solo	Sigh (1)
130		alto	Sigh (1)

The gentle affect of the *Pange Lingua* verses is contrasted to the stronger emotion of the verses for the unveiling of the Cross. The formal structure of the movement (ABABA) is clearly delineated by text, pitch focus, and timbre. The A sections are performed by solo soprano and low strings and are centered on the pitch C. The closing D-flat is heard as an unresolved note to C. The B sections are performed by the womens voices of the chorus and have a pitch focus on E. The A sections are written with legato contrapuntal lines; the B sections are more declamatory.

19.	*Dividentes vero vestimenta*	"And they parted his raiment"	Gospel narrative ("Father, forgive them") Text: St. Luke 23:34
M	*Text*	*Voices, Instruments*	*Musical Materials*
1		org	pedal C
2	Dividentes vero vestimenta eius miserunt sortes.	tenors	spoken together
4	Iesus autem dicebat	Evangelist	spoken
5	Pater	baritone (Jesus)	Sigh-inv (7)
6	Domine	full chorus	Domine (9)
7	dimitte illis	baritone (Jesus)	free melody, half steps and wide leaps
8	Pater	baritone (Jesus)	Sigh-inv (7)
9	non enim sciunt quid faciunt	baritone (Jesus)	free melody, half steps and wide leaps
10		vl	Święty Boże exp distributed-sustained
11		vl, vb, org	flurry legato, motives from CF-I (2) and CF-II (3)

As in movement 2, Penderecki uses the "Sigh-inv" motive each time Christ sings the word *Pater*. Penderecki reverses the order of events, placing the dividing of the raiment first and the forgiveness of Christ after this.

20.	*In pulverem mortis*	"Thou hast brought me into the dust of death"	A cappella Psalm Text: Psalm 22: 15-19
M	*Text*	*Voices, Instruments*	*Musical Materials*
1	In pulverem mortis	I alto	In-pulverem (23)
	deduxisti me	II alto	In-pulverem-inv (24)
4	deduxisti me	chorus	repeated D distributed-sustained
8		altos	repeated D antiphonal on vowels A O E
11	Foderunt	chorus	repeated 12-tone chords built from 3 diminished sevenths one half step apart
14	manus meas	chorus	ascending and descending minor ninths [sigh-inv. (7)]
18	Forderunt manus meas et pedes meos	chorus	descending half step lines, dissonant chords

M	Text	Voices, Instruments	Musical Materials
24	Dinumeraverunt omnia ossa mea	chorus	distributed-sustained and recited text
36	omnia ossa mea	men's voices	CF-II (3) (first four notes)
40	in	alto	In-pulverem-inv-retro (31)
	in pulverem mortis	bass	In-pulverem-retro (32)
42	ipsi vero considera-verunt et inspexerunt... Diviserunt sibi vesti-menta mea et super vestem meam mise-runt sortem.	chorus	Contrapuntal section based on Sigh (1), Sigh-inv (7)
51	Tu autem	chorus	descending minor sixths in octaves
52	Domine	altos	Sigh (1)
63	Tu autem domine ne elongaveris auxi-lium Tuum a me; ad defensionem meam conspice	chorus	Reciting and singing, building to a climax on a twelve-note chord
75	In pulverem mortis	I tenor	In-pulverem-inv (24)
	deduxisti me	II tenor	In-pulverem (23)

This movement begins with a literal repetition of movement 14 and then con-tinues with four more verses of the Psalm. The duet on *in pulverum mortis dedux-isti me* appears three times beginning in measures 1, 40 and 75 and serves as a frame for the two, roughly equal, halves of the movement. The dissonant twelve note chord formed of three o7 chords a half step apart on the word *foderunt* (pierced) recalls the use of the same chord at the end of no. 13 on the word *Crucifi-ge* (crucify).

21.	*Et stabat populus*	"And the people stood beholding"	Gospel narrative (mocking of Christ on the Cross) Text: St. Luke 23: 35-37
M	Text	Voices, Instruments	Musical Materials
1	Et stabat populus spectans, et deride-bant eum principes cum eis dicentes	Evangelist	spoken
2	?text? Alios salvos fecit	chorus	E-F (minor second)

M	Text	Voices, Instruments	Musical Materials
6		basses, tenors, percussion, contra-bassoon, str., basses	flurries, chorus imitates pizzicato sound
23	Alios salvos fecit	chorus	twelve note chords, divided text
		winds, brass, org	clusters
40	Alios salvos fecit	chorus	spoken, varied rhythms ending with a descending glissando whistle
		strings, percussion	flurries, strings play highest notes, pizzicato and also "behind the bridge" notes
48	si hic est	chorus	isolated spoken syllables
58	Christus Dei electus	chorus	chanted, various rhythms
53	Illudebant autem ei et milites accedentes et acetum offerentes ei et dicentes	tenors	recited
54	Si tu es rex Iudaeorum salvum te fac	chorus	octave G, then dissonant chords, fading to nothing

This is the first of three consecutive gospel narratives, each of which is focused on bringing out the meaning of the text cogently and effectively, more than on presenting musical ideas.

22.	*Unus autem de his*	"And one of the malefactors"	Gospel narrative (Jesus between the thieves) Text: St. Luke 23: 39-43)

M	Text	Voices, Instruments	Musical Materials
1	Unus autem de his pendebant latronibus, blasphemabat eum, dicens:	Evangelist	spoken
		chorus	12-note chord dying out
		low strings, fg	flurry
3	Si tu es Christus	basses	spoken
		chorus	yelled with glissando
		violins, piano, harm	cluster
	salvum fac temetip-sum et nos	basses	spoken

M	Text	Voices, Instruments	Musical Materials
4	Respondens autem alter increpabat eum dicens	chorus	spoken
6	Neque tu times Deum	bass (second thief)	spoken
7	quod in eadem damnatione es. Et nos quidem iuste, nam digna factis recipimus; hic vero nihil mali gessit... memento mei cum veneris in regnum Tuum	bass (second thief)	free melody of very small and very large intervals
		cr	dissonant chords
14		bass clar, contrabassoon, horn, trom	short passages accompanying voice
24	Domine	boys and tenors	Domine (9)
30	Amen dico tibi: Hodie mecum eris in paradiso	baritone (Jesus)	beings with "Sigh-inv" (7) and "Sigh" (1), leads up to high A
		altos	echo Amen half step higher
		org	legato slow line
35		cmb, hp, strings	unison A echos high A in baritone

Again the prime consideration is word setting. The closing high A on *paradiso* is but one of the highly effective text painting ideas in this movement.

23.	*Stabant autem juxta crucem*	"Now there stood by the Cross"	Gospel narrative (There stood by the Cross) Text: St. John 19: 25-27

M	Text	Voices, Instruments	Musical Materials
1		low winds, brass, string basses	pedal A^b
4	Stabant autem iuxta crucem Iesu mater eius et soror matris eius, Maria Cleophae et Maria Magdalene. Cum vidisset ergo Iesus matrem et	Evangelist	spoken

M	Text	Voices, Instruments	Musical Materials
	discipulum stantem, quem diligebat, dicit matri suae:		
7	Mulier, ecce filius tuus	baritone (Jesus)	free wide ranging melody
9	Deinde dicit disci-pulo:	Evangelist	spoken
10	Ecce mater tua.	baritone (Jesus)	free melody ending on G-A

The ending second G-A on the words *mater tua*, effectively prepares for the opening major second a^b-b^b in the *Stabat mater* (stood the mother) which follows directly.

24.	*Stabat mater*	"The mother stood"	A cappella chorus Text: sequence, *Stabat mater*
M	Text	Voices, Instruments	Musical Materials
1	Stabat mater	tenor I	Stabat mater (6)
2	Stabat mater dolorosa iuxta Crucem lacrimosa, Dum pendebat Filius	basses	unison A distributed text
16	Stabat mater dolo-rosa iuxta Crucem	altos basses	syncopated repeated a low dissonant chord
20	dum pendebat Filius	tenors	slow dissonant, syncopated chords
28	Quis est homo, qui non fleret, Matrem Christi si vederet In tanto supplicio?	chorus	a mixture of short isolated notes, falsetto repeated notes, long sustained notes ending with soft spoken words in various rhymes
57	Eia mater, fons amoris, me sentire vim doloris fac, ut tecum lugeam. Fac, ut ardeat cor meum in amando Christium Deum Ut sibi complaceam	chorus	contrapuntal treatment of Stabat mater (6) and Sigh (1) starting with one voice and ending with all twelve chorus parts
86	Christe	chorus	12-note chords, each chorus split into sixteen parts, notes arranged in fourths in each voice part

M	Text	Voices, Instruments	Musical Materials
87	Christe, cum sit hinc exire, Da per Matrem me venire ad palmam victoriae	altos	spoken like a litany
88	Christe	chorus	clusters in each chorus
89	Christe, cum sit hinc exire, Da per Matrem me venire ad palmam victoriae	chorus	spoken three-part canon
90	Christe, cum sit hinc exire	chorus	contrapuntal treatment of Stabat mater (6) and Sigh (1) motives
94	Christe, cum sit hinc exire Da per Matrem me venire ad palmam victoriae. Quando corpus morietur Fac, ut animae donetur paradisi gloria.	chorus	Alto Is sound the text in even notes on a repeated D while other parts sound sigh motives
105	Da per Matrem me venire	II bass	repeated Ds in syncopation in m
112	De per matrem me venire	III soprano	repeated Ds in faster syncopation building to a 10-note chord
116	Gloria	chorus	D major chord

This seminal work for the Passion has a clear structure delineated by the text and text setting.

1 A	Stabat mater	After the opening melodic line, the treatment is basically static
28 B	Quis est homo	A more active section rhythmically, but still static in terms of pitch motion.
57 C	Eia mater	Contrapuntal treatment, narrow range melodic lines
86 D	Christe	Spoken with some twelve note chords as incipits or interjections
90 E	Christe	This section first returns briefly to the melodic material and contrapuntal treatment of C and then continues with a variation of the static treatment of A.

The C section, as has already been mentioned, is incorporated into the opening movement, *O Crux, Ave* (measures 19-44). In the entire movement no melodic line ever exceeds a perfect fifth and most of the time the melodic lines remain within the range of a minor third. The emphasis on the whole step in the opening of the Stabat mater motive is in contrast to the emphasis on the half step which is typical for other motives of the *Passion*. The 10-note chord on *Paradiso* contains every pitch except F♯ and A, the third and fifth of the closing D major chord.

25.	*Erat autem fere hora sexta*	"And it was about the sixth hour"	Gospel narrative (The death of Christ) Text: St. Luke 23:44-46 St. John 19:30
M	Text	Voices, Instruments	Musical Materials
1		low strings, org	cluster with varied attacks
11		low winds, org	BACH (5), BACH-inv (4)
12	Erat autem fere hora sexta, et tenebrae factae sunt in universam terram usque in horam nonam. Et obscuratur est sol, et velum templi scissum est medium. Et clamans voce magna Iesus ait:	Evangelist	spoken
20		low brass	BACH (5), BACH-inv (4)
21		strings	quarter-tone cluster
26	Pater, in manus Tuas commendo spiritum meum	baritone (Jesus)	Sigh-inv, free melody
28		organ	CF-I-inv (13)
	consummatum est	boy soprano	CF-1-var. (33)

The previous settings of *Pater* (nos. 2 and 19) were all based on the "sigh-inv." motive, that is, on an ascending minor second. In this last cry to the Father, we hear the word set to the "sigh" motive, that is, to a descending minor second, perhaps suggesting the resignation and sorrow of Jesus. The words "consummatum est" are sung by boys' voices, a masterstroke that suggests it is no longer a particular mortal man speaking, but rather a universal immortal spirit.

The music of this movement is drawn directly from no. 18, measures 7-29 and 43-50, with the parts of the solo soprano and alto flute in no. 18 played by two violas in no. 26. The work acts as a brief moment of reflection following the death of Christ.

27.	*In te, Domine*	"In thee, O Lord"	Accompanied chorus Text: Psalm 31: 1-2, 5
M	*Text*	*Voices, Instruments*	*Musical Materials*
1	In pulverem mortis	II & III basses	repeated D
2	miserere	bass solo	BACH-retro (4)
6	Deus meus	baritone solo	Deus meus (8)
7	Crux fidelis	soprano solo	Sigh (1)
9	Stabat mater	I soprano	Stabat mater (6) (first two notes)
12	In te, Domine, speravi	boys chorus	In te (34)
	non confundar in aeternum	I tenors	non confundar (35)
14	In iustitia tua libera	soprano solo	CF-II (3), CF-I (2) (8 notes) then free melody
	miserere, in iustitia tua	baritone solo	BACH (5), CF-I (2) (6 notes) then free melody
15	miserere, iustitia tua libera me	bass solo	BACH-retro (4), CF-I-inv (13) (6 notes), then free melodies
17	Tua iustitia me	baritone solo	CF-II (3) (extra note at beginning)
19	In te, Domine, speravi	I chorus	In te-row (34)
20	Inclina ad me aurem tuam accelera me	full chorus	Deus meus (3), Deus-meus-inv (10) with other free contrapuntal lines
23	esto mihi in Deum protectorem et in domum refugii ut salvum me facias	full chorus	pedal A, sigh (1), sigh-inv (7)
37	In te, Domine, speravi	chorus	In te (34)

M	Text	Voices, Instruments	Musical Materials
38	In manus tuas commendo spiritum meum	boys	repeated D
	redemisti me	chorus	sustained-distributed leading to twelve note chord
40	Domine	boys and sopranos tenors	Domine (9)
41	Deus veritatis	full orchestra and chorus	repeated E major chords

This movement recapitulates many of the main melodic motives of the work, including various forms of CF-I and CF-II, BACH, the *Deus Meus* and *Stabat mater* and sigh motives. More subtle allusions may be also traced to the *Jerusalem* rhythm in the opening *In pulverem mortis*. The use of D as a reciting tone for repeated notes recalls the similar technique in the *Stabat mater*, no. 24.

The closing E major chord provides a sense of reassurance and hope at the end of this magnificent work.

Chapter VI

AN ANALYSIS OF PITCH RELATIONS

The analysis of the individual movements given in Chapter V would seem to indicate that the *St. Luke Passion* is based on a great variety of musical materials, and yet, as is the case with most great works of art, the listener is conscious of a strong sense of unity in this work. It is the purpose of this chapter to explore possible explanations for this sense of unity in terms of pitch relations.

Any discussion of similarities in pitch materials is subject to two possible types of errors. The first is to point out relations that may exist on paper or in an intellectual sense, but are not aurally perceptible. For example, it might be possible to relate the BACH (5) motive to the highest and lowest voices of the Domine (9) motive through processes of octave displacement, note exchange and transposition. Such a derivation, while feasible, would not be appropriate, especially when the composer himself has expressly labelled these as two different motives. Furthermore, the composer has on several occasions expressly denied his interest in complex manipulative processes that are more mental than aural.

The second danger is to point out relationships that are so general in nature that they exist not just among the particular melodic materials being studied in a given work, but among pitch materials in almost any work. An example of this approach would be to try to explain the entire *St. Luke Passion* on the basis of its use of the half step. It might be true that the half step does play an important role in the work, but it is just as true that half steps play an important role in countless other works of Penderecki and other composers.

The BACH and Święty Boże motives

In an attempt to avoid these two problems, two of the seminal motives of the work, the BACH motive and the Święty Boże motive, may be examined to see what contributes to the sense of relatedness that a listener finds in these motives, and yet explain it in such a way that it would not apply to a multitude of other works.

Ex. 6-1, Penderecki, *St. Luke Passion*, BACH and Święty Boże motives

     a) BACH   b) Święty Boże

An examination of these motives shows that they share two characteristics:
1. They do not use the same pitch twice.
2. They follow a pattern of melodic motion that can be described as a halfstep-leap-halfstep.

Both of these characteristics are aurally perceivable and both are sufficiently specific. They are, however, not unique to this work and in Chapter VII some other works with similar materials are cited.

Mod12 Integer Notation

In order to consider pitch relationships in greater detail, it will be helpful to introduce a special system of pitch and interval designation, known as Mod12 Integer Notation. It uses integers 0 to 11 instead of traditional pitch and interval names, as shown in Ex. 6-2. The pitch C is called 0, the pitch C♯ or D♭ is called 1, D is 2, D♯ or E♭ is 3, etc. In this system equal temperament is assumed and therefore there is no difference between two "enharmonic" pitches like C♯ and D♭, or D♯ and E♭.

Ex. 6-2, The Mod12 Integer Notation System

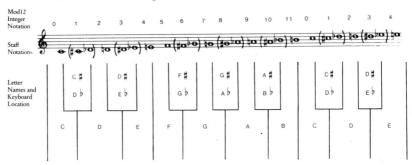

To find the interval between any two pitches, one simply subtracts the integer of the lower pitch from that of the higher pitch. For example, the interval between C and C♯ (or D-flat) is 1 (1-0=1); the interval between E and B-flat (or A-sharp) is 6 (10-4=6). In cases like the interval between A(9) and D(2) above it, where the number of the higher note is less than the number of the lower note, first add 12 to the higher note and then subtract the lower note from it:

$$2 + 12 = 14$$

$$14 - 9 = 5$$

The interval from A up to D is 5.

This process is actually the same as that involved in computing time intervals. The time interval between 9:00 a.m. and 2:00 p.m. is 5 hours, just as the pitch interval between 9 (A) and 2 (D) is 5.

Using integers for intervals makes it possible to express pitch relations in a simple way and makes the detection and description of pitch relations in a work like the *St. Luke Passion* easier than it would be using traditional pitch and interval designation. For example, the pitches and the pitch motion, or successive intervals, of the BACH and Święty Boże motives may be described efficiently using Mod12 Integer Notation as shown in Ex. 6-3.

Intervals BACH   Święty Boże

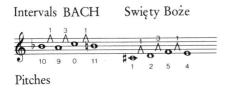

Pitches

It is possible to take a motive and *transpose* it, that is, move it to another pitch level. Using Mod12 Integer Notation, this process simply involves adding or subtracting the same number to each member of the motive as shown in Ex. 6-4. Transposing the two motives so they have the same lowest note makes it easy to compare them.

Ex. 6-4, Penderecki, *St. Luke Passion*, Transposition of BACH and Święty Boże motives

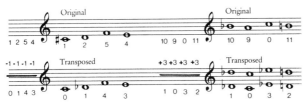

Pitch class set

Another concept that may help in the analysis of pitch relations is that of a *pitch class set*. A *pitch class* is a given pitch together with all of its enharmonic equivalents (i.e., different ways of spelling the same pitch) and its octave duplications. This is illustrated in Ex. 6-5.

Ex. 6-5, A Pitch Class Set

A *pitch class set* is an ordered collection of pitch classes; it may be labelled by listing the pitch classes it contains. For example: the pitch class set 0 1 2 3 contains the pitches 0 (C), 1 (C-sharp or D-flat), 2 (D), and 3 (D-sharp or E-flat). Pitch class sets are generally labelled in ascending order with 0 as their first member. They may be transposed to any other pitch location.[1]

Derivation of motives from a pitch class set

From a pitch class set it is possible to derive many different musical motives by arranging the pitches in various orders. To understand this concept it might be helpful to consider first a similar case with letters. The "letter set" A D E F could be used to form words such as FADE or DEAF or other combinations such as EFAD, DEFA, etc.

The application of this principle to music is shown in Ex. 6-6, which shows that several of the important motives in the *Passion* may be derived from the same pitch class set. The concepts of Mod12 Integer Notation, pitch class set, derivation of motives from a set, and transposition make it possible to represent in a single example many of the important relations between motives of the Passion. Example 6-6 presents the main pitch class sets used in the Passion. Following each pitch class set are the motives derived from it, presented with the lowest note as C so that they may be easily compared, and transposed to the pitch in which they appear in the motive table, that is, the pitch level on which they first appear in the Passion.

Ex. 6-6, Penderecki, St. Luke Passion, Main Pitch Class Sets

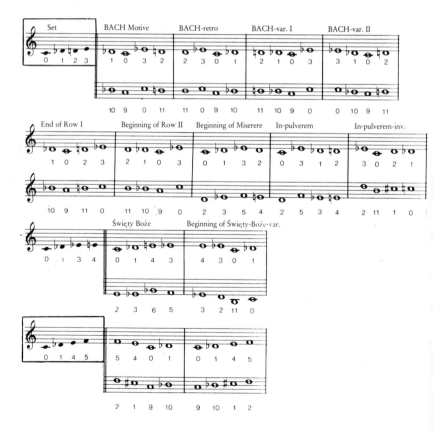

A study of Ex. 6-6 shows that all of the principal sets and most of the main motives in the Passion have interval 1 (halfstep) as the first and last interval, and that all of the motives avoid pitch class repetition. These are precisely the two characteristics discovered in the beginning of the chapter in the examination of the BACH and Święty Boże motives. The system of Mod12 integer notation permits an overview of the application of these characteristics to other materials.

It is important to remember that this is a way of making relationships easy to see, hear, and understand. It is in no sense an explanation of the way Penderecki composed. In an interview with the authors he indicated that his method of composing is first to find a melodic idea, then to sing it over, play it over, and finally to let it germinate in his mind for a period of time. Then he begins to compose and the materials flow from his mind to his pen in a way that he himself is not always able to analyze completely. This is in contrast to some other contemporary composers who engage in rigorous permutations of pitch materials according to highly specific pre-compositional practices.

The listener might emulate the composer's approach to his work at least to some extent. It is very helpful and interesting to play over the melodic motives given in Ex. 6-7 and try to learn to identify them. This kind of knowledge *of* the music, instead of knowledge *about* the music can lead to a deeper and more meaningful perception that goes beyond more superficial familiarity with the work.

Tone rows and serial composition

Arnold Schönberg (1874-1951) is generally credited with devising what he called "a system of composition in which the pitches are related only to each other." The essence of the system is to base an entire composition on various permutations and arrangements of a single 12-tone row or series. A 12-tone row, as used by Schönberg and others, is an ordered set of all 12 pitch classes with no pitch class repeated nor omitted.

The row may appear in 12 transpositions and four different forms – prime (P) or original form, inversion (I), retrograde (R) and retrograde-inversion (R-I). A strict twelve-tone composition is limited exclusively to these 48 possible forms for its pitch materials. Penderecki's *Passion*, like some compositions of Alban Berg (1885-1935) and others, is by no means a strict 12-tone composition. However, some techniques associated with 12-tone analysis may be helpful in studying this work.

One of the most valuable of these techniques is a matrix showing all 48 row forms in a compact fashion. In a matrix the original or prime form of the row (P) is read from left to right; the retrograde form of a row is read right to left, that is, in reverse order; the inversion form of any row is read from top to bottom; and the retrograde-inversion form from bottom to top. Ex. 6-7 shows the matrix for CF-I and for a twelve-tone row formed by combining CF-II and BACH.

In the matrices given in Ex. 6-7 the pitch class number 0 is always C, C♯ or D♭ is 1, D is 2, etc. The row in 6-7b may be regarded as being either 8 notes long or 12 notes long. The heavy lines within the matrix make it easy to find the eight note or four note forms. Intervals between successive notes of a row form are given outside the border of each matrix. These intervals may often be helpful when trying to locate a particular row. For instance, if a passage in the music has the interval structure of -1 +2 +1 -4 +1, it could come from the inversion of row II. On the other hand, a passage with the interval structure of +2 +5 -3, as in measure 58-59 of No. 18 in the cello, is clearly not derived from any row form since none of them has this particular sequence of intervals.

Ex. 6-7a, Penderecki, *St. Luke Passion*, Matrix Illustrating Świę ty Boże Motive Tone Row

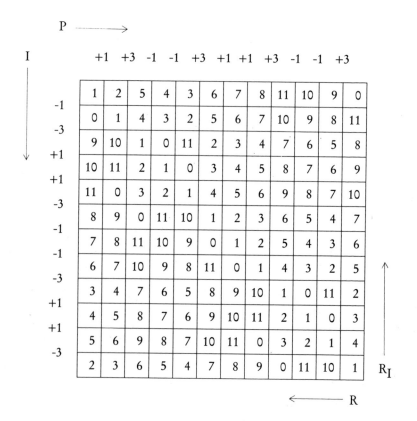

P ⟶

I

+1 +3 -1 -1 +3 +1 +1 +3 -1 -1 +3

1	2	5	4	3	6	7	8	11	10	9	0
0	1	4	3	2	5	6	7	10	9	8	11
9	10	1	0	11	2	3	4	7	6	5	8
10	11	2	1	0	3	4	5	8	7	6	9
11	0	3	2	1	4	5	6	9	8	7	10
8	9	0	11	10	1	2	3	6	5	4	7
7	8	11	10	9	0	1	2	5	4	3	6
6	7	10	9	8	11	0	1	4	3	2	5
3	4	7	6	5	8	9	10	1	0	11	2
4	5	8	7	6	9	10	11	2	1	0	3
5	6	9	8	7	10	11	0	3	2	1	4
2	3	6	5	4	7	8	9	0	11	10	1

Left intervals (top to bottom): -1 -3 +1 +1 -3 -1 -1 -3 +1 +1 -3

R$_I$

⟵ R

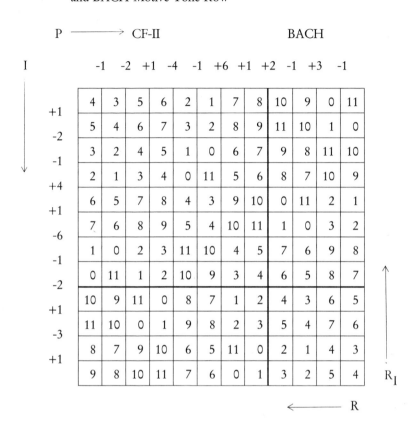

P ————→ CF-II   BACH

I   -1 -2 +1 -4 -1 +6 +1 +2 -1 +3 -1

+1	4	3	5	6	2	1	7	8	10	9	0	11
-2	5	4	6	7	3	2	8	9	11	10	1	0
-1	3	2	4	5	1	0	6	7	9	8	11	10
+4	2	1	3	4	0	11	5	6	8	7	10	9
+1	6	5	7	8	4	3	9	10	0	11	2	1
-6	7	6	8	9	5	4	10	11	1	0	3	2
-1	1	0	2	3	11	10	4	5	7	6	9	8
-2	0	11	1	2	10	9	3	4	6	5	8	7
+1	10	9	11	0	8	7	1	2	4	3	6	5
-3	11	10	0	1	9	8	2	3	5	4	7	6
+1	8	7	9	10	6	5	11	0	2	1	4	3
	9	8	10	11	7	6	0	1	3	2	5	4

R$_I$

←———— R

Other Pitch Relations

Closer examination of these "rows" reveals some interesting features. The first notes (sometimes called the first *hexachord*) of CF-I are transposed up by interval 6 to form the second six notes or hexachord.

Ex. 6-8, Penderecki, *St. Luke Passion*, First Hexachord of Cantus Firmus I in Analysis

1st hexachord   2nd hexachord
1 2 5 4 3 6   7 8 11 10 9 0

Another way of analyzing CF-I is to take the last note and put it an octave lower at the beginning. CF-I in this form is seen to be a series of ascending and descending three-note groups or trichords.

Ex. 6-9, Penderecki, *St. Luke Passion*, Cantus Firmus I in Trichords

The 12-tone row formed from CF-II and BACH may be analyzed as shown in Ex. 6-10:

Ex. 6-10, Penderecki, *St. Luke Passion*, the Pitch Materials of Cantus Firmus II and the BACH Motive in Analysis

CF-II var., which appears in No. 16, can be shown to be similar to CF-II-retro with the pitch F removed.

Ex. 6-11, Penderecki, *St. Luke Passion*, A Comparison of Cantus Firmus II Variation and Cantus Firmus II Retrograde

The BACH-row, which appears in No. 17, consists of three four-note groups or tetrachords; the first and last are BACH-retro motives, the middle is the BACH motive.

Ex. 6-12, Penderecki, *St. Luke Passion*, BACH Row in Movement 17

The "in te" motive begins with a four note pattern that is the same as the "in-pulverem inverted" pattern.

Ex. 6-13, Penderecki, *St. Luke Passion*, A Comparison of the *In Te* and *In Pulverem* Motives

All of these relations between motives in the Passion contribute to the perceived unity of the work. Other passages are related in more subtle ways. Many of the *flurries* are written with passages that seem to be based on one of the rows but depart from them in subtle ways. Perhaps they are best regarded as free creations based on characteristics of "halfstep-leap-halfstep" motion and no repeated notes, rather than on strict use of row forms. In a sense such passages bear the relation to a strict row passage that a handpainted design or mosaic does to a mechanically-generated design.

Other melodic materials

There remain other passages of melodic materials, especially the passages for the soloists, that seem to have no relation to the sets and motives discussed to this point. Indeed, the aural or visual effects of patterns such as those in Ex. 6-14 is clearly intended to contrast with that of the more closely related motives discussed to this point.

Ex. 6-14, Penderecki, *St. Luke Passion*, Contrasting Motives

However, closer study of this passage does show at least some subtle similarities to the other passages. The opening baritone solo may be taken as a case in point. The word "Pater" is sung to an inverted sigh motive. The next words "si vis" are sung to a large leap, but when considered as pitch classes, the motive would be a sigh motive. The G ♯ instead of appearing directly below the A is moved down one octave; this technique, which is called *octave displacement*, may be found not only in this work, but in other contemporary works. The remainder of the passage may be considered as being based on sets that are the same as or similar to those discovered earlier. The important point, however, is that Penderecki's approach here is even less subject to mechanical rules than it is in the places examined earlier. Penderecki simply seeks at all times the most appropriate expression for a given text in a given dramatic situation in the context of a given musical situation, relying on his musical imagination rather than on rigid precompositional procedures. For him, the ultimate criterion for the appropriateness of a given passage is not logical and intellectual but rather emotional and aural.

Notes

[1] For a full discussion of other conventions and concepts associated with pitch class sets, see Gary Wittlich, "Sets and Ordering Procedures," *Aspects of Contemporary Music*, (New York: Prentice Hall, 1975).

Chapter VII

A COMPARISON OF THE *ST. LUKE PASSION* WITH OTHER WORKS

All composers must face the task of reconciling the old and the new in their music; they must decide to which degree they wish to incorporate techniques and materials of the past in their works, or to what extent they must seek new solutions to compositional problems. Some, like the late-Romantics or neo-Classicists, have deliberately emphasized their links with the past; others, like the early futurists or later electronic composers and aleatory composers, have sought to emphasize what Milton Babbitt (b. 1916) has called "the jagged edge of abruption" between their music and the music of their predecessors. In most cases, whether consciously admitted or not, composers will move between these two extremes and in some cases they will achieve a magnificent synthesis of the old and the new.

This is the case with Penderecki and his *St. Luke Passion.* Manfred Schuler has said that the Passion reflects four musical epochs, the epochs characterized by melody, linear polyphony, harmony, and pure sound, and does it in such a way that "one can speak of a pluralistic musical consciousness of history . . . Familiar material is newly formulated, brought into new functional relations."[1]

It is the purpose of this final chapter to explore the relations between the Passion and other works of other composers and other works of Penderecki. No attempt will be made to chronicle every possible similarity to other works, but rather an attempt will be made to highlight those comparisons which seem to be most germane to the essence of the work. The chapter begins with larger aspects of form and texture and ends with a consideration of smaller aspects such as motivic relations.

Formal Aspects

Any comparison of the *St. Luke Passion* with other works would logically begin with works that Penderecki has openly acknowledged as influential in his thinking about the Passion setting – the two great Passions according to *St. Matthew* and *St. John* by Johann Sebastian Bach. In some ways the influence of these works might be said to be in a negative sense, some things were achieved so consummately in the *St. Matthew* and *St. John* Passions that the composer did not seek to emulate them in his *St. Luke Passion.* The most obvious evidence of this, one which was discussed in Chapter III, was the selection of a differnt Gospel text. However, there are several aspects of these Baroque masterpieces which were directly adopted or modified by Penderecki in his Passion.

The most significant of these is the large division of the work into two equal parts. Another is the division of the individual movements into those of report and reflection, into movements for the Evangelist which present the Gospel narrative, and movements for solo voice or chorus which present pious commentary upon the biblical narrative.

In both the Bach Passions and in the Penderecki Passion there are arias for solo voice. These are similar in that they involve more elaborate vocal lines than do the choral parts; they differ in that the Bach arias are mostly in the typical Baroque three-part *da capo aria* form (A B A or A B A') whereas the Penderecki arias are in a variety of forms ranging from free forms to rondo forms, but are never in what might be called a clear *da capo* aria form.

Most of the reflective choral sections of the Bach Passions are settings of Lutheran chorales, either in simple four part settings or more elaborate settings with solo sections. Some choral movements, like the magnificent closing chorus of the *St. Matthew Passion* are based on original poetry and music. The equivalent reflective choral sections in the Penderecki Passion are based on Psalms, Catholic hymns, or other biblical or liturgical sources.

Many writers have pointed out that the two Bach settings have different emphases, the *St. John Passion* is a tighter work with more emphasis on dramatic action and the *St. Matthew Passion* is a more expansive work with emphasis on contemplation. On the whole, the Penderecki Passion is regarded as being more in the tradition of the *St. John Passion* in its emphasis on action rather than contemplation, though it does come close to a balance of both elements.

Vocal Setting

In the choice of vocal forces the opening movement *of the St. Matthew Passion*, with its double chorus and (in the first chorus) single line added soprano part, may be said to have influenced Penderecki in his choice of triple chorus with two added high voices. The added voices in the Penderecki *Passion* are explicitly assigned to a boys chorus of soprano and alto; the added soprano line in the St. Matthew chorus is not specifically designated for boys' choruses but most writers on performance practice have stated that it would have been sung in Bach's time by boys' voices. In the famous 1829 performance of the Matthew passion conducted by Mendelssohn, the added soprano line was sung by women's voices.

The assignment of the words of Christ to a low male voice follows not only the Bach tradition but the earlier tradition of Plainsong Passions discussed in Chapter II. Similarly, the choice of chorus for the *Turba* is in keeping with historical tradition. Penderecki's use of a speaker rather than a singer for the words of the Evangelist is one of the most interesting aspects of the Passion. In some ways, this may be traced back to the earliest renderings of the Passion as a completely spoken text. It is generally in keeping with the idea that the Evangelist should appear in a middle range and moderate tempo to achieve the effect of neutrality or objectivity. The Evangelist is one who observes and reports events, not one who participates in the events or reacts to them.

Turning to Penderecki's technique for text settings, it is possible to find precedents for some of these in his own works and in those of other twentieth century composers and earlier composers. The concept of spoken text with musical accompaniment was called *melodrama* and can be found as early as the middle of the 18th century in works by Rousseau and Eberlin. Famous nineteenth century operatic examples occur in the dungeon scene of Beethoven's *Fidelio* and the Wolf's Glen scene in von Weber's *Freischütz*. *Sprechstimme* was used early in the 20th century by Humperdinck, Schönberg and Berg. Precedents for the technique of "distributed text" may be found in the medieval practice of "hocket" or in some canons of the English Baroque composers like Henry Purcell (1659-1695).

Instrumental Setting

The powerful drama of the Passion has often challenged composers to explore expanded instrumental resources. Bach in his *St. Matthew Passion* not only employs a relatively large instrumental ensemble for the time, but does it in a way that exploits many of the coloristic possibilities of the instruments, for example, the choice of the dark color of the oboe d'amore for "Ach Golgotha."

Even the continuo harpsichord, normally an unobtrusive background instrument, is used in unusual ways such as the tremolos and rapid scale passages in no. 73 where the words "rent the temple in twain" are set.

The use of the orchestra to set the scene in a dramatic work, as Penderecki does so effectively in such movements as nos. 5, 10, 13, 17, and 21, has precedents in such works as Franz Joseph Haydn's (1732-1809) oratorio, *The Creation*.

Turning to the influence of twentieth century composers on the instrumental settings of the Passion, one could cite the work of such composers as Edgar Varèse (1885-1965) as precedents for the instrumental timbres and techniques used in the Passion. More important, however, are the sound experiments that Penderecki made himself in the series of significant instrumental works that preceded the Passion. In works such as *Anaklasis, Polymorphia, Dimensions of Time and Silence, Threnody* and *Fluorescence*, Penderecki established the use of many of the techniques found in the Passion such as "clusters," "flurries," highest or lowest possible notes, and unusual ways of producing sounds with stringed instruments or voices. Indeed, in a televised interview in 1969, Penderecki said that with the composition of the *St. Luke Passion* he "stopped his search for new material. I had worked out my material in earlier works such as *Polymorphia* or *Threnody*. I then applied the experience that I had gained from these works to the composition of the *St. Luke Passion*."[2]

Gregorian Chant Influences

One of the most frequently discussed aspects of the *St. Luke Passion* is the possible influence of Gregorian Chant upon the melodic lines of the work. First of all, it should be established that there are absolutely no direct quotations in the work from any Gregorian melodies. As to the question of whether or not there were more indirect influences of Gregorian chant upon the composer, it would perhaps be best to quote the composer himself on this topic. In an interview with Tadeusz Zielinski, Penderecki was asked if he would agree with those who claimed that he was turning away from the present and trying for a deliberate archaic effect. Penderecki replied, "No, it is not a question here of 'archaisation' or stylisation, even if a deceptive impression of this may be given. On the contrary I was concerned with a clear expression of the text and a corresponding arrangement of the music; therefore maximum limitation of means and a certain expression of discipline and asceticism. That this produced effects which are similar to earlier music is a pure coincidence. The limitation of intervals to a minimum could be connected with the strictness of Gregorian Chant in its most primitive form. I was interested here in the aural shape of individual lines, clusters and stereophonic planes as well as the content of some words and sounds. For me these are just as much contemporary means as the ones I used in my other works; it is just that their selection was consciously limited. They can be derived from the essence of a cappella choral music (that should serve the text) in the same way as, for example, the means of *Threnody* were derived from the essence of instrumental music."[3]

This quotation makes it clear that Penderecki did not consciously intend to write a work "in the style of" Gregorian chant. However, it is still possible, as he indeed admits, to find striking similarities (deceptive though they may be) between the sound of movements, like the *Stabat mater* no. 24, and the sound of Gregorian Chant. A further interesting historic comparison is with the "neo-Gregorian Chant" of the Passions written by Heinrich Schütz (1585-1672) near the end of his life (see Chapter II).

Other pitch materials

Penderecki was by no means the first composer to pay homage to J. S. Bach by quoting his musical *soggetto cavato*. The B A C H theme has been used in such works as Robert Schumann, *Sechs Fugen über den Namen BACH*, op. 6; Franz Liszt, *Fantasie and Fugue on BACH*; Max Reger, *Prelude and Fugue on BACH*, op. 46; and Walter Piston, *Chromatic Study on the Name of Bach*.

The Święty Boże sets (0, 1, 3, 4) may also be found on other works. Here, however, it is not the case that these composers are deliberatly quoting this specific theme; indeed, it is doubtful if any of these other composers were acquainted with it. Rather, it is a case of using materials based on the same actual motive or on the same 0 1 3 4 set. Example 7-1 presents a selection of such related materials.

Ex. 7-1, Themes from other works that use the Święty Boże (0, 1, 3) set.

a) Bach, Well Tempered Clavier, Book I, Fugue in e minor

b) Copland, Piano Variations   c) Corelli, Concerto Grosso, op. 6 no. 11, III

d) Ravel, Rapsodie Espagnole, I

e) Stravinsky, Octet II

f) Mozart, Requiem, I m. 8

Re- qui- em ae- ter- nam

One other prominent motive which can be related to earlier music is the Domine motive (Ex. 7-2a). Wolfgang Martin Stroh has likened this to a medieval cadence pattern and Brunhilde Kaack has compared it to a Phrygian cadence pattern from Mozart's requiem (Ex. 7-2b). Here the use of the same text "Domine" makes the comparison even more cogent. Another way to relate this motive to earlier practice is to describe it as the simultaneous resolution of two incomplete augmented sixth chords.

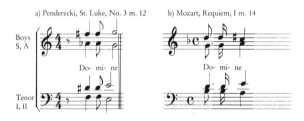

a) Penderecki, St. Luke, No. 3 m. 12   b) Mozart, Requiem, I m. 14

Boys
S, A

Do- mi- ne   Do- mi- ne

Tenor
I, II

Countless other comparisons with works of other composers or other works of Penderecki could be made. The opening quadruple octave G could remind listeners of the beginning of Beethoven's *Lenore Overture*, No. 3. The opening viola passage of the soprano Aria (no. 18) has been compared to the opening of Bela Bartók's *Music for Strings, Percussion & Celeste*. The soprano aria (no. 4) has some points of similarity with "Der Kranke Mond" from Schoenberg's *Pierrot Lunaire* or "L'artisan furieux" from Pierre Boulez' *Le Marteau sans Maitre*.

Undoubtedly further comparisons could be made; however, those cited establish the fact that this work of Penderecki has roots in earlier music. At the same time, however, it should be pointed out that this setting of the *Passion* points toward the future, not just in the sense of new and unusual techniques, but more importantly in the sense of a renewed emphasis upon expression of the text and communication with the listener.

It is this ability to find a language that is at once modern and traditional that has set Penderecki apart from other contemporary composers. When experimentation was necessary, he explored new sources of sound. When a synthesis was required, he turned to a more eclectic musical style. When the world-wide musical audience was beginning to tire of the avant garde, he developed a more expressive language. This characteristic of the music of Krzysztof Penderecki may account for the international success and recognition his works continue to receive, prompting Irving Kolodin to write:

> It is reasonable to say that the true character of a creator emerges when he can chart an esthetic vector between conflicting impulses, joining the best of both. Penderecki's possibilities permit us to reaffirm the magnitude of his endowment and to challenge him to find a new course. That would bring the most of which he is capable to a musical public desperately in need of it.[4]

Notes

[1] Manfred Schuler, "Tonale Phänomene in Pendereckis 'Lukas-Passion,'" *Melos/Neue Zeitschrift für Musik* 2, no. 6 (1976):460.

[2] Karl Josef Müller, *Informationen zu Penderecki's 'Lukas-Passion'*; *Schriftenreihe zur Musikpädagogik*, (Frankfurt am Main: Diesterweg, 1973):17.

[3] Tadeusz A. Zielinski, "Der zeitgenössische Komponist und die Tradition," *Ruch Muzyczny* no. 22 (1963).

[4] Irving Kolodin, "Penderecki's Progress," *World* 2 (August 14, 1973).

**Im Rahmen der Siebenhundertjahrfeier
des dritten Domes zu Münster**

Mittwoch, 30. März 1966, 20 Uhr
im Dom zu Münster

Krzysztof Penderecki

Passio et mors
Domini nostri Jesu Christi
secundum Lucam
Passionsmusik nach Lukas
für Sopran-, Bariton- und Baßsolo,
Sprecher, drei gemischte Chöre,
Knabenchor und Orchester

Kompositionsauftrag des WDR
Uraufführung

Mitwirkende:
Stefania Woytowicz, Sopran
Andrzej Hiolski, Bariton
Bernard Ładysz, Baß
Rudolf Jürgen Bartsch, Sprecher
Der Tölzer Knabenchor
Einstudierung: Gerhard Schmidt
Der Kölner Rundfunkchor
Chordirektor Herbert Schernus
Das Kölner Rundfunk-Sinfonie-Orchester
Leitung: **Henryk Czyż**

Die Uraufführung wird gleichzeitig im Dritten Programm des Westdeutschen Rundfunks übertragen

Stefania Woytowicz, soprano; Andrzej Hiolski, baritone; Bernard Ładysz, bass; Leszek Herdegen, narrator. Krakow Philharmonic Symphony Orchestra and Chorus, Henryk Czyż, conductor; Polish Gramophone SXL 0325/6, Philips 802 771/72AY.

Stefania Woytowicz, soprano; Andrzej Hiolski, baritone; Bernard Ładysz, bass; Rudolf Jürgen Bartsch, narrator, Tölzer Boys Choir, Cologne Radio Orchestra and Chorus, Henryk Czyż, conductor; RCA VICS-6015; BASF JA 293 793 (Harmonia Mundi).

SELECTED BIBLIOGRAPHY

Books

Erhardt, Ludwik. *Contemporary Music in Poland*. Translated by Eugenia Tarska. Warsaw: Polonia Publishing House, 1966.

Erhardt, Ludwik. *Spotkania a Krzysztofem Pendereckim*. Krakow: Polskie Wydawnictwo Muzyczne, 1975.

Jarocinski, Stefan, editor. *Polish Music*. Warsaw: Polish Scientific Publishers, 1965.

Müller, Karl Josef. *Informationen zu Pendereckis 'Lukas-Passion'; Schriftenreihe zur Musikpädagogik*. Frankfurt am Main: Diesterweg, 1973.

Müller, Karl Josef. "Krzysztof Penderecki (1933), Aus den 'Psalmen Davids' für gemischten Chor und Instrumental-Ensemble (1958)." (p. 201-233) *Perspektiven Neuer Musik* Mainz: Schott, 1979.

Robinson, Ray. *Krzysztof Penderecki: A Guide to His Works*. Princeton: Prestige Publications, Inc., 1983.

Schwinger, Wolfram. *Penderecki: Begegnungen. Lebensdaten, Werkkommentare*. Stuttgart: Deutsche Verlagsanstalt, 1979.

Vogt, Hans. *Neue Musik seit 1945*; Stuttgart: (Reclam, 1972), p. 347-360.

Periodicals

"A Krakkoi Filharmonia egzuettesenek ket hangversenze." *Muzsika* 12 (November 1969), p. 4.

Bachmann, Klaus Henning. "Alpbach–Venice–Warsaw." (in English, German and French) *The World of Music* 11, no. 1 (1969), p. 55.

Berthelson, Bertil. "Penderecki paa scenen." *Musikrevy* 25, no. 3 (1970), 129-130.

"Buenos Aires wird mit neuer Musik überschüttet." *Melos* 37 (May 1970), p. 201.

Bürde, Wolfgang. "Berlin: Alban Berg's 'Lulu'–Krzysztof Penderecki's 'Lukas Passion.'" *Neue Zeitschrift für Musik* 129 (April 1968), p. 185.

Calcaneo, Maria de Los Angeles. "Desde il verano y el otono europeos." (including a summary in English on page 47) *Heterofonia* 2, no. 9 (1969), p. 30.

Chlopecki, Andrzej. "'Pasja' Pendereckiego jako znak." *Ruch Muzyczny* 19, no. 4 (1975) p. 3-5.

Cohn, Arthur. "Two Recordings of the Penderecki Passion according to St. Luke." *American Record Guide* 31 (April 1968), p. 624-626.

Douglass, Robert. "Choral Performances." *American Choral Review* 12 (July 1970), p. 120-123.

Duck, Leonard. "The Manchester Scene." *Musical Opinion* 103 (July 1980), p. 404.

Erhardt, Ludwik. "A Glance at Contemporary Musik in Poland." *Polish Music* 12, nos. 1-2 (1979), p. 22-24.

Felder, David and Schneider, Mark. "An Interview with Krzysztof Penderecki." *The Composer* 8 (1976-1977), p. 8-20.

Fierz, Gerold. "'Die Lukaspassion' von Krzysztof Penderecki – ein Vergleich zweier Aufnahmen." *Schweizerische Musikzeitung* 107, no. 5 (1967), p. 299-300.

Fleming, Shirley. "Musician of the Month Krzysztof Penderecki." *High Fidelity/Musical America* 25 (December 1975), MA p. 6-7.

Flummerfelt, Joseph. "'Passion According to St. Luke' Penderecki." *Choral Journal* 13 (April 1973), p. 7-12.

Frankenstein, Alfred. "Penderecki: 'St. Luke Passion.'" *High Fidelity/Musical America* 19 (May 1969), MA p. 21-22.

Geraedts. Jaap. "De 'Lukas-Passie' van Penderecki." *Mens en Melodie* 21 (July 1966), p. 196-198.

Golea, Antoine. "'La Passion selon Saint Luc' de Krzysztof Penderecki." *Journal Musical Francais* 66 (February 1968), p. 33-34.

Gori, Gianni. "Trieste: Penderecki 'Passion' staged." *Opera* 31 (June 1980), p. 591-2.

Grzenkowicz, Isabella. "Conversations with Krzysztof Penderecki." *Polish Music* 12, no. 3 (1977), p. 24-30 and no. 4 (1977), p. 10-14.

Hempel, G. "Warschauer Herbst 1966." *Musik und Gesellschaft* 16 (December 1966), p. 849.

Henderson, Robert. "Music in London." *The Musical Times* 108 (July 1967), p. 624.

– "Penderecki's 'St. Luke Passion.'" *The Musical Times* 108 (May 1967), p. 422.

Herbort, H. J. "Klänge und Klagen." (Reprinted from *Die Zeit*, 23 February 1968) *Das Orchester* 16 (April 1968), p. 185.

Hugli, Pierre. "'La Passion selon de Saint Luc' de Krzysztof Penderecki." *Revue Musicale de Suisse Romande* 20, no. 2 (1967), p. 14-15.

Jacobsen, Bernard. "Penderecki – a mighty vote from Poland." (recording) *High Fidelity/Musical America* 17 (April 1967), p. 74-75.

Jaksic, Djury. "Varsavska jesen po deseti put." *Zvuk* no. 70 (1966), p. 718-720.

Kaack, Brunhilde. "Pendereckis Zwölftonreihe – Versuch einer Interpretation des Eröffnungschores der Lukas Passion." *Musica* 29, no. 1 (1975), p. 9-15.

Koegler, Horst, "Düsseldorf." *Opera* 20 (June 1969), p. 525-526.

– "Düsseldorf." *Opera News* 33 (14 June 1969), p. 25.

– "Pendereckis 'Lukas Passion' szenisch." *Musica* 23, no. 3 (1969), p. 366.

Kolodin, Irving. "Music to my Ears." *Saturday Review* 52 (22 March 1969), p. 69+.

– "Penderecki's progress." *World* 2 (14 August 1973), p. 42-43.

– "The Passions of Penderecki." *Saturday Review* 51 (24 February 1968), p. 63-65.

Krellmann, Hanspeter. "Novy Penderecki." *Hudebny Rozhledy* 19, no. 11 (1966), p. 350-351.

– "Pendereckis 'Lukas Passion' szenisch: Uraufführung an der Düsseldorfer Oper unter Henryk Czyz." *Neue Musikzeitung* 18, no. 2 (1969), p. 2.

"Leipzig: Penderecki's 'Lukas-Passion.'" *Musik und Gesellschaft* 29 (January 1979), p. 20.

Lowe, Steven. "Bach Collegium ınd Kantorei Stuttgart." *High Fidelity/Musical America* 19 (January 1969), MA p. 11.

Lüttwitz, Heinrich von. "Düsseldorf." (scenic version) *Neue Zeitschrift für Musik* 130 (May 1969), p. 216-218.

– "Pendereckis grosse 'Lukaspassion': Uraufführung des WDR im Dom." *Neue Zeitschrift für Musik* 127 (May 1966), p. 186-187.

Lüttwitz, Heinrich von."Penderecki – Passion in sechs Städten." *Das Orchester* 26 (May 1978), p. 401-402.

Meyer-Janson, B. "Pendereckis 'Lukas Passion' in Hamburg." *Musik und Kirche* 40, no. 5 (1970), p. 356-357.

Müller, Karl Josef. "Informationen zu Penderecki's 'Lukas-Passion'; Schriftenreihe zur Musikpädagogik." (Book Review) *Musikhandel* 25, no. 3 (1974), p. 169.

– "Informationen zu Pendereckis 'Lukas-Passion'; Schriftenreihe zur Pädagogik." (Book Review) *Musik und Bildung* 7 (January 1975), p. 39.

Müllmann, Bernd. "Hersfeld." *Neue Zeitschrift für Musik* 130 (May 1969), p. 214-216.

– "Siegfried Heinrichs Einstudierung von Krzysztof Pendereckis Lukas Passion in Hersfeld." *Das Orchester* 17 (June 1969), p. 261-263.

Münstermann, Hans Jochen. "Düsseldorf macht szenische Experimente mit Pendereckis 'Lukas Passion.'" *Melos* 36 (June 1969), p. 262-263.

Muggler, Fritz. "Zürich während der Juni-Festwochen." *Melos* 26 (October 1969), p. 441.

Musielak, H. "Le Xe Festival de musique contemporaine de Varsavie." *Journal Musical Francais* 57 (May 1967), p. 26-27.

Mycielski, Zygmunt. "'Passio et Mors Domini Nostri Jesu Christi Secundum Lucam' Krzysztofa Pendereckiego." *Ruch Muzyczny* 10, no. 10 (1966), p. 3-7.

Nestler, Gerhard. "Dreimal Penderecki." *Melos* 35 (December 1968), p. 469-470.

– "Neues vom Klang." *Melos* (September 1968).

"Neu und interessant." *Musikhandel* no. 4 (June 1967).

"New York." *Music and Artists* 2, no. 2 (1969), p. 30.

Newell, Robert. "'Passio' – Structure and Performance." *American Choral Review* 16 (July 1974), p. 13-19.

Niehaus, Manfred. "Krzysztof Penderecki 'Lukas-Passion' – eine Schallplattenaufnahme." *Neue Zeitschrift für Musik* 128 (March 1967), p. 113-114.

Orga, Antes. "Exaggerated Passion." *Music and Musicians* 16 (October 1967), p. 36-37.

– "Krzysztof Penderecki." *Music and Musicians* 22 October 1973), p. 38-41.

– "Penderecki: composer of Martyrdom." *Music and Musicians* 18 (September 1969), p. 34-38.

– "'Saint Luke' for Moderns." *Music and Musicians* 15 (May 1967), p. 28+.

Page, Frederick. "Warsaw." *The Musical Times* 107 (December 1966), p. 1079.

"Passio Domini Nostri Secundum Lucam." *Ruch Muzyczny* 13, no. 4 (1969), p. 11.

"Passio et Mors Domini Nostri Jesu Christi Secundum Lucam." *National Symphony Program Notes* (17-19 April 1973), p. 29A-30A.

Patton, Harold. "Penderecki, Composer for the Last Judgement." *Chicagoland and FM Guide* (April 1969), p. 37.

"Penderecki's 'St. Luke Passion.'" *Musical Events* 22 (July 1967), p. 28.

Pfannkuch, Wilhelm. "Pendereckis 'Lukas Passion' in Kiel." *Musik und Kirche* 39 (May/ June 1969), p. 132.

Pirckmayer, Georg. "Avantgarde 1970." *Musikerziehung* 24, no. 4 (1971), p. 148+.

Quinke, J. "'Lukas-Passion' von Penderecki." *Musik und Kirche* 26 (may/June 1966), p. 143-144.

– "Pendereckis 'Lukas-Passion.'" (Kassel) *Musica* 20, no. 3 (1966) p. 119-121.

– "Pendereckis 'Lukas-Passion.'" *Musica* 23, no. 3 (1969), p. 271-272.

Romano, Jacobo. "La 'Passion' de Penderecki." *Buenos Aires Musical* 24, no. 394, (1969), p. 2.

Sadie, Stanley. "Editorial." *The Musical Times* 108 (September 1967), p. 793.

"Salzburger Festspiele 1970." *Oper und Konzert* 8 (September 1970), p. 8-9.

Schoor, Dieter. "Stuttgarter Kirchenmusiktage." *Musik und Kirche* 38 (March/April 1968), p. 85-86.

Schuhmann, C.R. "Konzerte." *Oper und Konzert* 10, no. 5 (1972), p. 41-42.

Schuler, Manfred. "Tonale Phänomene in Pendereckis 'Lukas-Passion.-" *Melos/Neue Zeitschrift für Musik* 2, no. 6 (1976), p. 457-460.

Schwinger, Wolfram. "Pendereckis 'Lukas Passion.'" Stuttgart) *Musica* 22, no. 1 (1968), p. 15-16.

Siwek, Marian. "Pasja w Teatrze Wielkim." *Ruch Muzyczny* 23, no. 6 (1979), p. 11.

"Skrowaczewski, Minnesota give 'Passion' top reading." *Billboard* 81 (22 March 1969), p. 38.

Spingel, Hans Otto. "Journal des Monats." *Opern Welt* no. 6 (June 1969), p. 13.

Steger, Hellmuth. "Pendereckis 'Lukas Passion.'" *Musica* 22, no. 5 (1968), p. 357-358.

Stilz, Ernst. "Pendereckis 'Lukas Passion' – Versuch einer Gegenüberstellung mit Teilen der Matthäus Passion von Bach." *Musik und Bildung* 2 (July/August 1970), p. 319-325.

Stroh, Wolfgang Martin. "Penderecki und das Hören erfolgreicher Musik." *Melos* 37 (November 1970), p. 452-460.

Stuckenschmidt, Hans Heinz. "Polnische Passion im Dom zu Münster." *Melos* 33 (May 1966), p. 152-155.

Tomasek, Andrija. "Vise od obicnog koncerta." *Zvuk* no. 91 (1969), p. 47-48.

Wiese, K. M. "Bleibt die Gemeinde draussen vor der Tür?" 27. Nürnberger Orgelwoche. *Gottesdienst und Kirchenmusik* no. 4 (July/August 1978), p. 126-127.

Weißstein, Curt B. "Buenos Aires." *Neue Zeitschrift für Musik* 130 (July/August 1969), p. 349.

– "Premiere sud-Americaine de las "Passion selon de Saint Luc' de Krzysztof Penderecki." *Revue Musicale de Suisse Romande* 22, no. 3 (1969), p. 20.

White Chappel. "Choral Performances." *American Choral Review* 12 (October 1970), p. 197-199.

Young, Percy. "Report from England." *American Choral Review* 10 (Winter 1968), p. 73-74.

"Z sal koncertowych." *Ruch Muzyczny* 20, no. 24 (1976), p. 10-11.

Theses (Unpublished)

Gebuhr, Ann Karen. "Stylistic Elements in Selected Works of Krzysztof Penderecki." (Unpublished Masters degree thesis, Indiana University, Bloomington, Indiana, 1970).

Hutcheson, Robert Joseph, Jr. "Twentieth Century Passion Settings: An analytic Study of Max Baumann's *Passion*, Op. 63; Frank Martin's *Golgotha*; Krzysztof Penderecki's *St. Luke Passion*; and Ernst Pepping's *Passionsbericht des Matthäus*." (Unpublished Ph. D. Thesis, Washington University, St. Louis, Missouri, 1976).

Linthicum, David Howell. "Penderecki's Notation: A Critical Evaluation." (Unpublished DMA thesis, University of Illinois, Urbana-Champaign, 1972).

Bürde, Wolfgang G. "Leiden von Auschwitz." *Der Tagesspiegel* (Berlin), 20 February 1968.

"Das Kühnste – gerade kühn genug." *Der Feuerreiter* (Köln), 30 April 1966.

"Die *Lukas-Passion* von Krzysztof Penderecki." *Neue Zürcher Zeitung*, 15 April 1966.

"Ein großes Ereignis." *Buersche Zeitung*, 1 April 1966.

"Eine neue Lukas-Passion im Dom zu Münster." *Ruhr-Nachrichten* (Dortmund), 1 April 1966.

"Ein Pole in Münster." (Interview) *Kölnische Rundschau*, 1 April 1966.

"Eine Uraufführung in Westfalen." *Carrefour* (Paris), 6 April 1966.

Ekiert, Janusz. "Bach als Leitmotiv." *Die Presse (Wien), 4 April 1966.*

– *"Penderecki's Lukas Passie." Het Parool* (Amsterdam), 2 April 1966.

"Genutzte Chance." *Polen*, 9 September 1966.

"Gregorianik und Geräuschekstasen." *Main-Echo* (Aschaffenburg), 7 April 1966.

Henahan, Donal. "Religiously a Free Spirit. Politically?" *New York Times*, 16 March 1969.

Herbort, Heinz Josef. "Belehrung aus Polen." *Die Zeit* (Hamburg), 4 April 1966

– "Klänge und Klagen." *Die Zeit* (Hamburg), 23 February 1968.

Hiemenz, Jack. "A Composer Praises God as One Who Lives in Darkness." *New York Times*, 27 February 1977: Sec. 2, D19&D36.

"Holland - Festival 1967." *Neue Zürcher Zeitung*, 15 July 1967.

"Im Auftrag des WDR: Die Lukas-Passion von Penderecki." *Kirche und Rundfunk* (Köln), 6 April 1966.

"Im Dienst der Aussöhnung." *Freie Presse* (Bielefeld), 2 April 1966.

Joachim, Heinz. "Bericht und Bekenntnis." *Die Welt* (Hamburg), 20 February 1968.

Kaiser, Joachim. "Passion eines Verzweifelten." *Süddeutsche Zeitung*, 2 April 1966.

Kirchberg, Klaus. "Ein Abbild des Leidens." *Westdeutsche Allgemeine Zeitung* (Essen), 1 April 1966.

Kirchmeyer, Helmut. "Passion aus Polen." *Kölner Stadtanzeiger*, 15 April 1966.

"Klang- und Geräuschekstasen im Dom." *Die Rheinpfalz* (Ludwigshafen), 6 April 1966.

Klare, Wolfgang. "Geniales Werk kongenial interpretiert." *Münsterische Zeitung* (Münster), 2 April 1966.

Krellmann, Hanspeter. "Golgotha in Auschwitz." *Reutlinger Nachrichten*, 2 April 1966.

– "Golgotha und das Lied der Welt." *Generalanzeiger Wuppertal*, 2 April 1966.

– "Passion aus Polen." *Die Welt*, 4 April 1966.

– "Passion der Versöhnung." *Wiesbadener Kurier*, 2 April 1966.

– "Polnische Lukas-Passion." *Mannheimer Morgen*, 2 April 1966.

"Lass mein Rufen in Deine Ohren dringen, Herr, vernimm mein Schreien." *Kirche und Leben*, 4 April 1966.

Lüttwitz, Heinrich von. "Pendereckis Passion." *Rheinische Post* (Düsseldorf), 1 April 1966.

– "Pendereckis Passion." *Badische Zeitung* (Freiburg), 2 April 1966.; *Weser-Kurier* (Bremen), 2 April 1966.; *Badische Neueste Nachrichten* (Karlsruhe), 6 April 1966.

"Mit kompositorischen Mitteln unserer Zeit." *Fuldaer Zeitung*, 5 March 1966.

Müllmann, Dr. Bernd. "Ein leidenschaftlicher Klagegesang." *Hessische Allgemeine*, 1 April 1966.

"Musikalische Uraufführung in Münster." *Münsterische Zeitung*, 3 March 1966.; *Badische Volkszeitung* (Karlsruhe), 4 March 1966.; *Tagesanzeiger* (Regensburg), 8 March 1966.

"Passion in neuer Klangwelt aus dem Geist unserer Zeit." *Siegener Zeitung* (Siegen), 6 April 1966.

"Penderecki Lukaspassie Midden in Deze Tijd." *Arnhems Dagblad*, 1 April 1966.

"Polnische Uraufführung in Münsters Dom." *Neue Rhein-Zeitung*, 1 April 1966.

Rockwell, John. "San Francisco Debut of 'Passion.'" *Oakland Tribune*, 13 January 1969.

Rohrer, Bob. "Symphony Performs Penderecki." *Atlanta Constitution*, 20 March 1970.

Rothärmel, Marion. "Lukas-Passion: Ein gewaltiges Glaubensbekenntnis Pendereckis." *Kölnische Rundschau*, 1 April 1966.

Schnoor, Dr. Hans. "Polnische Passion." *Westfalen Blatt* (Bielefeld), 3 April 1966.

Schonberg, Harold C. "Romanticism Coming Up?" *New York Times*, 16 March 1969.

Schreiber, Ulrich. "Wunder im Dom." *Der Mittag* (Düsseldorf), 1 April 1966.

Schürmann, Hans G. "Im Zeichen der Christlichen Hoffnung auf Versöhnung." *General-Anzeiger* (Bonn), 1 April 1966.

Schwinger, Wolfram. "Das Meisterwerk." *Stuttgarter Zeitung*, 3 June 1967.

– "Die Polnische Passion." *Stuttgarter Zeitung*, 14 November 1967.

Strongin, Theodore. "An Avant-Garde Passion." *New York Times*, 2 July 1967.

Stuckenschmidt, Hans Heinz. "Polnische Passion." *Frankfurter Allgemeine Zeitung* (Frankfurt), 4 April 1966.

Sucher, C. Bernd. "Der Avantgardist – und was aus ihm wurde." *Schwäbische Zeitung Leutkirch*, 10 May 1979.

"Uraufführung im Dom zu Münster." *Kasseler Post*, 1 April 1966.

"Vorstoff zum Neuen Klang." *Christ und Welt*, 3 June 1966.

Wasita, Ryszard. "Avantgarde und Erbe." (Interview) *Zeitschrift Aus Polen*, July 1966.

Wendland, Jens. "Neue Kirchenmusik aus Polen." *Hannoversche Allgemeine Zeitung*, 4 April 1966.

Ziegler, Karl Kurt. "Lukas-Passion in Neuer Klangwelt." *Westfälische Rundschau* (Münster), 1 April 1966.